Enhancing Democratic Systems:
The Media in Mauritius
A Dialogue Session

Edited by

Christina Chan-Meetoo
&
Roukaya Kasenally

Langaa Research & Publishing CIG
Mankon, Bamenda

Publisher
Langaa RPCIG
Langaa Research & Publishing Common Initiative Group
P.O. Box 902 Mankon
Bamenda
North West Region
Cameroon
Langaagrp@gmail.com
www.langaa-rpcig.net

Distributed in and outside N. America by African Books Collective
orders@africanbookscollective.com
www.africanbookcollective.com

ISBN: 9956-727-19-9

Table of Contents

Acknowledgements

The editors and organisers of the 2010 National Dialogue Session on 'Enhancing Democratic Systems: The Media in Mauritius' wish to thank the following organisations and people for having provided support for the initiative:

- the UNESCO for sponsoring the event and publication,

- the UOM for logistical support and hosting,

- the participants who agreed to present and submit a paper,

- the persons who spontaneously agreed to chair the various sessions, namely, Amadou Mahtar Ba, Ibrahim Koodoruth, Sheila Bunwaree and Caroline Ng Tseung Wong.

- the people who attended the sessions and participated in discussions,

- the media who reported on the conduct of the conference,

- the two conference assistants, Danessa Seenayen and Pravin Meetoo,

- the Mediacom Studio technician Ketan Ramhit,

- Enrico Chadien for his pictures,

- Azhagan Chenganna for help in the logistical aspects,

- and all UOM staff who have helped in the organisation.

Introduction

The National Dialogue Session on 'Enhancing Democratic Systems: The Media in Mauritius' was held on the 16th and 17th September 2010 at the University of Mauritius as a joint collaboration between the Communication Studies Unit and UNESCO. The main objective of this dialogue/conference was to provide a forum to discuss certain key issues related to the media in Mauritius; with an added emphasis on the role of the media in society, policy and regulation, relationships with the political sphere, industry trends and training issues.

The different panel themes of the conference attracted the presence and participation from a number of key stakeholders: media practitioners, regulatory institutions, political parties, civil society and academia. This led to fruitful exchanges and sometimes passionate debates, more particularly in the sessions devoted to politics and the media. One can only conclude that such opportunities for healthy discussions need to be a regular feature on the local scene, especially when these relate to areas perceived as sensitive. Creating the necessary space to engage into dialogues of such nature are important as they 'depassionate' charged and tensed environments which often can be detrimental to the proper functioning of the media. In fact, the present proceedings are being published with a view to more widely disseminate the content of presentations and discussions of the conference and help further 'clear the air'.

The papers compiled in this publication follow the order as per the programme of the dialogue session so as to keep the same relevant thematic groupings. Where indicated, some papers were transcribed from audio recordings of the presentations when the speakers could not send their own extended version in writing.

Opening Session and Keynote

The opening session which was chaired by Christina Chan-Meetoo, Lecturer in Media and Communication and co-convenor of the conference, started with general introductions by the Acting Vice-Chancellor of the University of Mauritius, Associate Professor Daneshwar Puchooa and, the Dean of the Faculty Professor Sanjeev Sobhee who both praised this initiative. These were followed by a special address by the keynote speaker Amadou Mahtar Ba, CEO of the African Media Initiative. In his paper, Amadou Ba stressed on the importance of a strong, independent and professional media in a democracy and spoke in favour of self-regulation in the industry. The keynote speaker recognised that the media may at times err but strongly believed that a properly self-regulated media is crucial for the public good.

Session 1: Freedom, Media and Democracy

The first plenary session chaired by Ibrahim Koodoruth, Senior Lecturer in Sociology, was devoted to the theme 'Freedom, Media and Democracy' with presentations by practicising journalists and editors as well as a legal expert. The latter, Maneesh Gobin, emphasised the place of freedom of expression in the Mauritian Constitution as well as in the various International Conventions on Human Rights, and how these offer opportunities for the media. He also evoked the existence of legal and systemic constraints to this freedom. In his presentation, Subash Gobine, Senior Editor at the Defi Media Group, explained the formal and informal measures used by the government to intimidate the press whilst acknowledging the challenges posed by media ownership.

Gilbert Ahnee, editor-in-chief at La Sentinelle, was unfortunately unable to submit a complete paper. However his summary communication stressed on the fact that we do live in a democracy, not a dictatorship and that journalists often have shortcomings and should beware of corporate communication that can often corrupt the true nature of journalism. Finally, journalist Catherine Boudet, a former academic, referred to what she calls 'containment' strategies by the state on the public sphere and the difficulty for media practitioners to fulfil a real critical and analytical role.

Second 2: Media Systems and Policies

The second session entitled 'Media Systems and Policies' saw presentations from representatives of the state television, private commercial radio, academia, regulatory institutions and industry associations. The first part of this session was chaired by the keynote speaker Amadou Mahtar Ba. In his speech, Dan Callikhan, director of the MBC, offered justification for the new management style at the broadcasting station whilst alluding to the conflictual relationship with the Ministry of Labour. Abdoollah Earally, a radio journalist, insisted on the need for more balance in the local mediascape, when it comes to hard news/soft news, audience participation, and in commercial aspects of the industry. In her paper, Roukaya Kasenally, Senior Lecturer at the University of Mauritius and co-convenor of the conference, referred to the changing mediascape both globally and locally and questioned the role of the MBC as public broadcaster which she believes behaves more like a state broadcaster.

In the second part of this session which was chaired by Roukaya Kasenally, the Chairman of the IBA Complaints Committee Gilbert Ithier explained the procedures for complaints with respect to media coverage by radio stations and how the Complaints Committee which is a tribunal deals with hearings and adjudications. Lindsay Rivière, Chairperson of the Newspapers Editors and Publishers Association, recalled the history of codes of ethics in the Mauritian media industry and presented the newly approved code of ethics published by the industry association. Finally, in her paper, Christina Chan-Meetoo, Lecturer at the University of Mauritius, outlined the major sources of tension between the press and government and advocated for self-regulation with a strong participation from ordinary citizens.

Session 3: Media, Politics and Democracy

The third session dedicated to 'Media, Politics and Democracy' was chaired by Sheila Bunwaree, Professor in Sociology and focused on presentations from mainstream political parties as well as extra-parliamentary groups and academia. In his presentation, Cehl Fakeemeeah, Member of Parliament and Leader of the Front Solidarité Mauricien (FSM), argued in favour of diversity in the media as well as privatisation of the national television station the MBC. Steven Obeegadoo, Member of Parliament and spokesperson for the opposition party the Mouvement Militant Mauricien (MMM), stressed on the need for the State to respect the press, for the media to be professional and responsible, for liberalisation of television to happen sooner than later and finally for barriers to monopoly to be lifted. Nita Deerpalsing, Member of Parliament and spokesperson for the ruling party the Labour Party (LP), asked the audience to reflect on the commercial nature of the media and referred to the expression 'zero-sum game' for the current conflict between government and the press, more particularly with the Sentinelle Group. This session generated great interest from the audience and the parliamentarians present were queried about the real commitment of their respective parties, about reforms in nomination procedures for regulatory authorities, and about the forthcoming Media Commission Bill.

The second part of the session opened with the intervention of Nilen Vencadasamy of Blok 104 who recalled the history of this extra- parliamentary group and how the press has helped them gain public visibility and credibility in their fight against communalism in the electoral system and Constitution. For Ashok Subron, spokesperson for Rezistans ek Alternativ, extra-parliamentary forces are as crucial to democracy as are the media in order to challenge the status quo. Finally, in her paper, Mayila Paroomal, Senior Lecturer at the University of Mauritius, provided an overview of the important roles the media play in ensuring the conduct of 'free and fair elections' and made a case for monitoring the media during election time.

Session 4: Citizens and the Media

The fourth session entitled 'Citizens and the Media' was chaired by Caroline Ng Tseung Wong, Senior Lecturer in Psychology, and had presentations by a representative of regulatory authorities in ICT, a media practitioner, a citizen blogger/computer scientist and an academic. In his presentation, the director of the Independent Communication Technology Authority (ICTA), Krishna Oolun, evoked the need for a multi-stakeholder approach in determining regulatory policies. The editor-in-chief of *L'Express-Dimanche*, Rabin Bhujun, compared citizen journalism with professional journalism and argued that they are not in competition with each other. Rather, the journalist who blogs can leverage the features of the web 2.0 for better interaction, accountability to readers and powerful storytelling.

Avinash Meetoo, Director of Knowledge Seven and citizen blogger argued that citizen journalism can help compensate for the dysfunctional educational system, encourage innovative thinking and ultimately bring about a better society. He examined open systems such Wikipedia and AgoraVox and elections.mu (which he created) and advocates self policing on the web. Finally, Azhagan Chenganna, Lecturer at the University of Mauritius, charted the role of new media in activism and social transformation and made reference to the structural constraints which hinder such development.

Round Table: Challenges to the Trade in Training and Professionalism The final session chaired by Christina Chan-Meetoo was a round table on the 'Challenges to the Trade: Training and Professionalism' with the participation of a number of practitioners from the media. In his presentation, Kiran Ramsahaye, editor-in-chief of *Le Matinal* recognised the weaknesses in the profession. Whilst stating that many practitioners in the industry do not necessarily have any training and yet deliver professionally, he felt that formal and dedicated training would help hoist up the standards.

In his paper, Jean-Claude de l'Estrac, Chairman of *La Sentinelle*, stated that the profession must live up to the challenging transformation of the industry and argued in favour of the rise of the new term 'journanalyst' whilst acknowledging the difficulties in adequately rewarding these new 'intellectual' workers. He also reiterated his belief in the need for self- regulation as referred to a commissioned report in 1999 by the Media Trust and which unfortunately had not received the support from the various media operators.

Henri Marimootoo, senior journalist at *Week-End*, highlighted the fundamental distinction between communication and journalism, for which he thinks training should be completely separate. He outlined the many weaknesses in the profession in terms of training and advocated for the setting up of a regional school of journalism to raise the standards. Finally, Axcel Cheney and Jean-Luc Emile, two radio journalists, both observed that training opportunities are scarce in the field and felt this situation has not helped maintain rigorous standards within the profession.

In conclusion, this national dialogue session in the media has, for the first time, brought together media practitioners from different media houses as well as other key stakeholders. It has demonstrated that a non partisan venue such as the University of Mauritius with the esteemed patronage of the UNESO can provide a space for level-headed exchanges. Contrary to popular beliefs, there are no fundamental oppositions, merely differences in points of views. These can be easily overcome as the general consensus is undoubtedly that the media are a crucial feature to our democracy. Generally, existing forms of regulation are seen as an important component to provide an adequate and reasonable framework for media practice. But in the face of impending state regulation which is still taking a long time to materialise, it is widely agreed that regulation should ideally take the form of self-regulation to ensure transparency and accountability first and foremost to the public, not merely to the government. Training is also believed to be essential so as to upgrade the standards in the profession and avoid the pitfalls of amateur, spineless or sensationalist journalism as well as to meet the challenges posed by new media trends.

The Concept Note

Enhancing Democratic Systems the Media in Mauritius: A Dialogue Session The concept note

An unfettered, independent and objective media is considered to be the guardian against any form of abuse, discrimination or malpractice in society. UNESCO's celebration of World Press Freedom Day this year with the theme *Freedom of Information: The Right to Know,* has highlighted the importance of freedom of information as an integral part of freedom of expression and its contribution to democratic governance. Celebrated as the Fourth Estate in many established and emerging democracies, the media has acquired formidable power and authority to influence or control events and shape opinions. However, what has been termed in certain quarters as the unbridled power/influence of the media brought in demands to control, regulate and put under greater scrutiny the latter.

This saw the setting up in a number of countries of dedicated regulatory bodies and media councils backed and sponsored by either governments or manned by the media practitioners themselves who felt it was more to their advantage to opt for self-regulation than be imposed what they termed as the heavy handedness of governmental bodies. The experience with different forms of regulation has been varied depending on the manner in which the concept was implemented in respective countries and whether regulation in the medium to long term did contribute towards building a more responsible, fair and equitable society. In fact, these different regulatory country experiments act as an important repertoire of information in terms of good practices for countries faced with similar regulatory demands.

The Noughties has for its part opened up unimaginable opportunities with the advent of new media. New media has in fact challenged the traditional and established sources of power and authority namely the state and media producers/owners and increasingly tilted the balance in favour of the average citizen. Although still in its early stage of growth, citizenship journalism supported by new technology has the capacity to create an important societal, political and cultural shift causing democratic revolutions even in the most closed, controlled and undemocratic regimes. The last decade has witnessed a host of new social platforms that have inherently transformed the world of media; the case of the 'Green Revolution' in Iran following the May 2009 election offers a compelling example.

Africa has been faced with similar considerations especially with the advent of democratisation that has swept across the continent. In the case of Mauritius, the media is relatively well established (nearly 250 years of print media, 60 years of broadcast and 7 years of private radio stations presence) and has always been considered an important feature of the Mauritian democratic model. However, it is important to emphasise on the fact that the print and broadcast media follow two very different traditions – one which is highly unregulated and in the hands of private owners whilst the other state owned/controlled. It is only in the recent years (2002 onwards) that private commercial radio stations started broadcasting on the island. Regulation remains a highly contentious and charged issue – especially when it comes to that of the print media. As for the broadcast media, legislation was enacted in 2000/2001 and saw the setting up of regulatory bodies - the Independent Broadcasting Authority (IBA) and the Information and Communication Technologies Authority (ICTA). Despite their presence, a number of observers have commented on their limited scope of intervention and lack of independence from political parties in power.

The proposal for the setting up of a press complaints committee can be traced to 1999 with the commissioning of the Kenneth Morgan Report by the Media Trust and more recently the current Prime Minister commissioned Professor Geoffrey Robertson to draft a Media Commission Bill. The idea of regulation (imposed or self) has been a source of unease and tension and till date matters are still unresolved with on one side the government threatening to impose regulation across the board (through its Media Commission Bill) and individual initiatives of certain media groups to set up their own regulatory and complaints body.

On the other hand, the absence of a Freedom of Information Act and the prevailing culture of secrecy within the civil service (due to the severe threat of severe disciplinary action against public officers who communicate with the press and the existence of the Official Secrets Act) represent a severe lacuna which impedes the proper functioning of the media as information channel and as watchdog in the Mauritian democratic setup.

Therefore the aim of this conference is through a dialogue session to allow the key stakeholders to:

1. Take stock of the existing battery of legal and regulatory framework with respect to the media in Mauritius.

2. Revisit the various debates/exchanges about the changing role of the media in a democracy.

3. Examine the relationship between the media and the different institutions such as the government, regulatory bodies and civil society.

4. Explore the good practices available in the area of media regulation/self regulation.

5. Engage into dialogue with key stakeholders in relation to the above and ensure a way forward for its prompt implementation.

Through this dialogue session, we also hope to build upon existing work already done such as the 2008 UNESCO-IPDC Media Development Indicators[1] or the 2008 African Barometer report for Mauritius[2] and to synergise efforts towards an enhanced democratic system that strikes the right balance between freedom of information or expression and media governance.

---

[1] Available at: http://unesdoc.unesco.org/images/0016/001631/163102e.pdf

[2] Available at: http://www.fes-madagascar.org/media/pdf1/AMB%20Mauritius%202008%20English.pdf

Welcome Remarks

Professor Sanjeev Sobhee
Dean of the Faculty of Social Studies & Humanities

Acting Vice-Chancellor: Associate Professor Puchooa CEO Africa
Media Initiative: Mr Amadou Mahtar Ba
Colleagues of the UOM
Distinguished guests
Ladies and gentlemen

It is with immense pleasure that I welcome you all to this dialogue
session on this very pertinent and topical issue 'Enhancing
Democratic Systems: the Media in Mauritius'.

This is very much in accordance with Unesco's celebration of
the World Press Freedom Day's theme 'Freedom of Information: the
Right to Know'.

While conventionally the role of the media was confined to
informing people on various aspects of the society, today its scope
has much broadened to becoming a catalyst for economic progress.

In a document known as the Washington Consensus which
helped to shape the economies of several countries in the 1990's, it
was clearly laid down that the institutional environment is
paramount to economic development and that very environment
encompasses the media. We have today data on freedom of the
press, voice and accountability that constitute key variables when
addressing the progress of economies.

However, from a historical perspective, it is important to note
that there could be heated debates between the media and
democracy across the world. Our country bears no exception to this
tendency. It is thus imperative ladies and gentlemen that there is a
dialogue that reasserts time and then the various issues involved and
their implications. Freedom of expression involves indeed very often

regulation. To what extent must the media be regulated is a debatable issue. But whatever we do should not frustrate the thirst for knowledge, distort the actual role of the media or impede our democratic systems.

Thus aptly chosen today is the debate organised by colleagues of the Communications Unit that will take stock of what has been achieved so far in the media and democracy world and what are the features that need to be looked/relooked into to ensure the right balance between freedom of expression and media governance.

As you might have observed the various sessions involve an impressive list of different stakeholders and representatives to ensure that this is so.

I wish you well and hope that you will have very fruitful interactions with productive outcomes.

Thank you.

Opening Speech

Associate Professor Daneshwar Puchooa
Acting Vice-Chancellor, University of Mauritius

Warm greetings to everyone! Welcome to the University of Mauritius who is indeed happy to partner with the UNESCO through its Eastern Africa cluster on this important two-day dialogue session. I understand from the two co-conveners of the conference, Mrs Chan-Meetoo and Dr Kasenally, that the term 'dialogue' was privileged from the onset so as to reflect the nature and dynamism of the debates and discussions over the next two days; with the aim of hopefully building consensus and a common agenda for the enhancement and consolidation of democratic systems.

In fact, this dialogue session is quite opportune as it comes at a time of tension between a section of the media and those in power. We sincerely hope that the dialogue session can help towards creating better dialogue and exchanges between the various stakeholders.

Glancing at the dialogue programme, I am quite impressed that a number of key stakeholders (media practitioners, regulatory bodies, public media institutions, elected members of parliament, members of the civil society and academics) will be engaging each other as panelists and participants. In fact, getting such a diverse and enlarged group to devote their time, energy and intellectual capital is indeed a feat which the University of Mauritius is proud to be part of. Indeed, this reflects the role and responsibility that an institute of higher learning like ours must promote – offer a platform/space for new ideas to be formulated, diverse exchanges to be encouraged and debates to be engaged. Here I am reminded of the wise words of the fine intellectual Edward Said, who called upon academics/intellectuals to be at the forefront of the shaping of progressive ideas and debates.

At this point, I would also like to thank the Eastern Africa cluster of UNESCO who has been partnering with the Media and Communication Unit of the University of Mauritius on a number of projects such as the setting up/financing of a Media Communication Lab and of which the holding of today's dialogue session is the latest one. We, at the University of Mauritius strongly believe in partnership as it offers us with apt opportunities of building more relevant and meaningful projects that allow us to remain in sync with the changing world of industry, business and society.

I would like to thank the keynote speaker, Mr Amadou Mathar Ba, who is the CEO of the African Media Initiative for making time from his hectic schedule. No doubt, his keynote address will pave the way for the discussions over the next two days.

Last but not least, I would like to thank the two co-conveners of the workshop, Dr Kasenally and Mrs Chan-Meetoo, who have given a fair amount of their time, energy and intellect to bringing the dialogue session to fruition. I understand that there is still more work for them as an important outcome of the two day dialogue session is to produce the proceedings of the conference which is expected to act as a sort of blueprint for the way forward.

Therefore allow me to wish you all a fruitful and enriching exchange of ideas over the next two days and thank you for your attention.

Keynote Speech

Amadou Mahtar Ba
CEO African Media Initiative (AMI)

Greetings, I am so glad to be here this afternoon in this temple of knowledge to discuss what I believe is one of the most important components of open societies: the existence of a free, independent, ethical and professional media.

It is truly an honour to be among like-minded individuals who share in the recognition that the media remain a central pillar in building strong democracies, economies, and societies.

Quite frankly though, talking about such a serious subject in such a beautiful country as Mauritius while we can go enjoy the sun and the beach is not necessarily my preference. Dr Kasenally that is the reason why I hesitated before accepting to be here today.

Let me start my remarks by clearly stating that I am not an academic and therefore please forgive me if I use a more casual language compared to what you are used to hearing at the university.

Having said that, I, however, think I can contribute by sharing my personal perspectives – those of an African media executive who has spent several years in the private media sector in Africa and in the USA and who is continuing to work toward reshaping the future of the African media landscape through an international non-profit institution called the African Media Initiative (AMI).

Ladies and gentlemen, dear friends and colleagues, in delivering his opening address to the Ghanaian Parliament in July 2009, President Barack Obama stated what most of us here if not all would applaud. He said: "An independent press is part of the capable, reliable and transparent institutions that will lead Africa to success in the 21st century."

I believe this is one of the most powerful statements President Obama made during his trip to Africa as President of the United

States. It is a statement on which all Africans and friends of the continent must build to push the agenda for a friendlier environment for media development.

Since President Obama gets it, what can we do to help ensure that his policies follow this vision? What can we do to ensure that other world leaders also recognize the importance of an independent press and then facilitate its emergence and support it?

So friends, what do we know? What makes so many policy makers around the world, academics and other thinkers believe that media play such a crucial role in enhancing our democratic systems? Let us look around the world and try to understand why.

In 1842 Latin America, a revolutionary named Simon Bolivar declared that the masses need to be educated using public debates, newspapers and books.

In the United States, in 1787, Thomas Jefferson, the third American President, boldly declared: "The basis of our governments being the opinion of the people, the very first object should be to keep that right; and were it left to me to decide whether we should have a government without newspapers or newspapers without a government, I should not hesitate a moment to prefer the latter".

In London, in 1900 at the first Panafrican Congress led by W.E.B. Dubois the famous African American visionary, the first decision taken was to build a panafrican news network to help educate the world about the living conditions of black people and particularly those in Africa under colonial domination. Sixty three years later, in Ethiopia, at the creation of the Organization of African Unity (OAU) the ancestor of today's African Union, the founding leaders, in their first declaration, called for exactly the same thing. The OAU decision led to the creation of the Panafrican News Agency, PANA, years later as an Intergovernmental organization where I started my professional career in the media sector by helping restructure and privatize it.

In Asia, the Economics Nobel Prize winner Amartya Sen argues in his book *Poverty and Famine* that no country with multi-party politics and free media has ever suffered from famine.

So, that is what we know, and through all these examples, what is striking is throughout history, many thinkers asserted that the media are an essential public good. The media can accomplish civic education and provide people with knowledge of their rights, duties and safeguards. Through media, whether community radio stations, local newspapers or television programmes, especially in local languages, it is possible to develop the most remote areas. All these possibilities, including building linkages among different cultural and ethnic groups, are the foundation of our nations.

Let me put it even more strongly by making an analogy with the human body: if the lungs are essential to the health of the body, it is the oxygen which they process which is the key to life. The media is the oxygen of the body politic when we talk of good governance, accountability and democracy. You can have all the vital organs: heart, brain, and liver but without oxygen the body shuts down and dies.

Similarly democracy needs elections, parliament, separation of powers, a vibrant civil society and a private sector. But without the media, democracy in modern societies and economies just cannot work.

It becomes then as if around the world, visionary leaders have supported the view that the media has a special role in our societies and therefore deserve protection from any type of hindrance, and particularly from any form of government censorship and regulation. After all, press freedom results from the longstanding view that the media help us find the truth - often by holding government representatives and others accountable for crimes, corruption and ineptitude. The media can also help us identify their achievements and successes, a role which is sometimes conveniently forgotten.

We have many examples to demonstrate the key role of media in enhancing democracy.

For instance, in early 2000, at the highest point of the conflict in a country of Francophone West Africa (which though we are among friends, will remain nameless to protect the guilty), I visited the head of state. I thought that I could be helpful in convincing him to release two public radio journalists arrested for reporting about the unrest in the country. I also wanted to talk to him about releasing the funds promised to support the nascent vibrant private media.

After listening to me very carefully, he only had one question "Why would I help feed the monster that wants me out of my seat"? Since that day, I have come to strongly believe that it is a fallacy to think that dictators do not know the importance of the role media can play. I believe that, in fact, it is exactly because they know and understand the media well that they choose to crack down on this sector. It is also that knowledge and understanding that drives leaders of *coups d'état* to always secure radio and TV stations right at the onset.

Second example: Has anybody seen the documentary movie *"Pray the Devil Back to Hell"*? Its about the Liberian Peace Talks in Accra in 2003 mediated by Nigerian General and former head of state Abdusalami Abubakar.

The movie demonstrates the role of women peace activists in forcing rebel leaders and government officials to reach a peace agreement. These fearless women used radios and cell phones to target and mobilize other women to converge onto the meeting venue, blocking all exit doors so that no one could leave the negotiations until an accord was signed.

Third example. Most recently, many journalists have been jailed in the aftermath of the disputed elections results in Iran. When President Ahmedinejad was asked about it in an interview with NPR while visiting the UN headquarters in New York, he said that to his knowledge no journalist was in jail because of their reporting negatively on him or his government and he asked for names. Less than a week later, the journalist mentioned in the interview was released.

Through these examples, we can see the role of the media as well as information and communication technologies in building strong democracies based on justice and equality.

But if we all know this argument, and accept it, what are we doing to help strengthen media in the places where it is most needed?

Let me emphasize that strong independent media does not occur in a vacuum. A society also needs other strong institutions, the judiciary in particular.

For this reason, I challenge all of us here to start thinking about the holistic nature of media and of media development. We must all become advocates within the private sector, development institutions, development partners and our own governments about the necessity to focus greater attention to the media sector.

Innovative efforts which look to include media front and centre in global efforts to promote democratic governance and accountability need to be given much higher priority.

BECAUSE...

First and foremost, a strong, independent and professional media are central to achieving and maintaining good governance and accountability and all the positive good that stems from having responsible and accountable authority. Media are irreplaceable public watchdogs providing a platform for a well informed citizenry to endorse or sanction its leaders.

In addition, media that perform their watchdog role, making government actions transparent, can help spur economic development overall by making it more difficult for public funds to be wasted in unnecessary projects or disappear from state coffers into the pockets and accounts of a few.

Second, a strong, independent and professional media help build confidence for economic investment by signalling that impunity has no place in the system.

Third, a strong, independent and professional media is a source for credible information in areas as vast and different as health matters, environmental concerns, cultural events, entertainment, and the list goes on.

Friends, if this is true, then we face another challenge. That we must recognize much of the investment in media in Africa thus far has yielded poor returns. While they sometime look good on paper, many of the programs to support media development over the years have not given us the results we would have hoped. The figure of about 250 to 300 million dollars being spent annually on media development is probably a conservative estimate. But what do we have to show for this investment?

Allow me here to mention the example of the African Media Initiative (AMI) which I believe is an innovative and holistic way to secure strong and independent media across the continent so that it can effectively help promote democratic governance and accountability, economic development and human progress.

This initiative, inspired by the Commission for Africa recommendations on the eve of the G8 Summit in Gleneagles, was developed following the largest ever consultation and research process on the media in Africa, under the auspices of the UN Economic Commission for Africa and the BBC World Service Trust. It concluded that there is significant public and private underinvestment in Africa's media sector and that efforts need to be of greater scale and strategic focus.

AMI research and consultation specifically found that:

- *Despite sector growth, professionalization is patchy with standards low and training programs tending to be static, short-term and lacking impact.*
- *Little to no attention is paid to business and management training.*
- *The changing technology landscape is both a huge opportunity and a black hole of knowledge for most media houses and practitioners.*
- *Accreditation systems are still used as political tools by governments.*
- *Enabling environments for free media and for increased private investment oftentimes are inconsistent and remain restrictive.*

These findings represent serious problems for anyone concerned about enhancing democratic systems, governance and accountability of our nations.

As demonstrated by the AMI research and consultation, accepted values and roles for the media based on global best practice or even the formally agreed policies of the AU are not well rooted. The media's operation is susceptible to both external and internal controls (state pressure, regulation, and control; as well as the use of private media to pursue narrow or hidden political, religious, or ethnic goals).

To address these core constraints, AMI defined a vision of an African media that is pluralistic, largely sustainable, free and responsive to the needs and interests of its audiences.

AMI believes that while state/public media and community media remain critical, it is the private media which will drive the media and information revolution in Africa. AMI will focus on the importance of fostering and supporting leadership standards to implement agreed policies and ethical practices across the sector and emphasising the fundamental importance of improving economic sustainability through new revenue streams, investments and adapting to changing technologies.

I would love the opportunity to talk more about AMI with those interested.

For now, let me return to the topic of the day.

All the examples I have evoked reassure us in our beliefs that media play a critical role in building democracy, support economic growth and remain a pillar of our societies. But having said that, we must not sit back and rest on our laurels in this knowledge.

Haven't we seen media play a negative, indeed destructive role too? Do we not have examples of that?

Indeed, I have discussed the positive role of media but there are too many examples, from Rwanda to Zimbabwe, Kenya, Guinea and Somalia, where media have participated in unleashing the devils and showing the worst part of human nature. We all know the devastating role played by *Radio Mille Collines* in the genocide in Rwanda, the role of ethnic radio in Kenya in inciting post election violence, and the use of radio, Internet, and media technologies by al-Shabaab in perpetuating violence throughout Somalia.

We are not here today to expand on these and other "worst practices." However, I really do believe that we have to learn from these sad lessons. We must consider them as loud calls to vigorously embark on serious long term and strategic focus on the media. We must avoid repeating the worst chapters of our collective history.

I opened with the words of past and present leaders from around the globe who all spoke of the important role of the media in building democratic and successful nations. On the American soil, over two hundred years separate Jefferson from Obama and both view media as a sine qua non condition for building strong democracies and societies.

Yet, even with centuries of experience, venerable American media institutions are under siege, not having figured out how to harness new media technologies. The same scenario is developing on our continent where we are witnessing large media houses become almost irrelevant to the benefit of very small ventures (sometimes no more than 3 people) that have perfected the use of new information and communication technologies, the mobile phone in particular.

While these new technologies open up and enlarge the media space, it is crucial to pay sustained attention to the professionalism and ethics in the sector as a whole, new and traditional media alike.

This poses the important debate about regulation of the media sphere and the tendency in many African countries to move from voluntary self regulating media council systems to statutory media appeals bodies, including in democratically advanced countries like South Africa.

I profoundly believe that a self regulatory mechanism with an Ombudsman capable of ordering a correction or an apology anytime a media is found guilty is far more effective than a statutory mechanism which imposes heavy fines and jail terms. Indeed the Ombudsman, says Raymond Louw, Chairman of the Press Council of South Africa, strikes at the heart of a news organisation's operations. By publishing a correction and an apology, readers and the audience at large are told that the media was not only inaccurate but that it behaved unprofessionally or even dishonestly.

In my view, nothing damages a newspaper more than a ruling against its credibility and trustworthiness. If the public loses its trust in a news organization it inevitably goes out of business, thus enduring the ultimate sanction.

I want to close by insisting that in establishing or enhancing democratic systems we must not fall into the easy path of advocating for regular elections, or even setting up pseudo separate powers alone. A much broader view is needed. A view in which independent, professional and ethical media have a central place. And it is our common duty to frame that view and advocate for it. After all, let us keep in mind that elections represent a key moment in both conflict resolution and conflict escalation. So without an informed citizenry, thanks to free and professional media, elections alone are not helpful.

In concluding, I could not find a better place to meditate on the question about what makes the coffee sweet than here in Mauritius - Is it the sugar or is it the act of stirring it?

Likewise, let us ask ourselves what makes democracy work? Is it having elections or an independent and professional media? I believe that what makes our societies sweet and the best way of enhancing our democratic systems is having a media that can periodically stir the pot while at the same time ensuring that it can uncover the best and the worst of our societies.

I look forward to listening to your bright ideas over the course of the next two days. If we are successful in Mauritius and on this continent in enhancing our democratic systems through media, I am sure that we will learn best practices that can be employed worldwide.

I thank you all very much.

Constitutional and Legal Frameworks Opportunities and Constraints for the Media Industry in Mauritius

Maneesh Gobin Barrister-at-Law

Thinking about opportunities and constraints for the media industry in Mauritius, I can do no better than to start by reproducing Section 12 of the Constitution of Mauritius[1] :-

12 Protection of freedom of expression

(1) Except with his own consent, no person shall be hindered in the enjoyment of his freedom of expression, that is to say, freedom to hold opinions and to receive and impart ideas and information without interference, and freedom from interference with his correspondence.

(2) Nothing contained in or done under the authority of any law shall be held to be inconsistent with or in contravention of this section to the extent that the law in question makes provision –

(a) in the interests of defence, public safety, public order, public morality or public health;

(b) for the purpose of protecting the reputations, rights and freedoms of other persons or the private lives of persons concerned in legal proceedings, preventing the disclosure of information received in confidence, maintaining the authority and independence of the courts, or regulating the technical administration or the

---

[1] The Constitution of Mauritius is the "…supreme law of Mauritius…" and if any other law is inconsistent with it then that other law "…shall, to the extent of the inconsistency, be void" – Section 2 of the Constitution.

technical operation of telephony, telegraphy, posts, wireless broadcasting, television, public exhibitions or public entertainments; or

(c) for the imposition of restrictions upon public officers, except so far as that provision or, as the case may be, the thing done under its authority is shown not to be reasonably justifiable in a democratic society.

I reproduce now Article 10 of the European Convention of Human Rights:

Article 10 Freedom of expression

1. Everyone has the right to freedom of expression. This right shall include freedom to hold opinions and to receive and impart information and ideas without interference by public authority and regardless of frontiers. This Article shall not prevent States from requiring the licensing of broadcasting, television or cinema enterprises.

2. The exercise of these freedoms, since it carries with it duties and responsibilities, may be subject to such formalities, conditions, restrictions or penalties as are prescribed by law and are necessary in a democratic society, in the interests of national security, territorial integrity or public safety, for the prevention of disorder or crime, for the protection of health or morals, for the protection of the reputation or rights of others, for preventing the disclosure of information received in confidence, or for maintaining the authority and impartiality of the judiciary.

The purpose of reproducing these two articles is to highlight the very same ambit of the "freedom of expression" under our Constitution and the European Convention – i.e as *"…freedom to hold opinions and to receive and impart information and ideas without interference…"*

It is important to highlight that Mauritius gained independence in 1968. It is widely accepted that the constitutional "father" of Mauritius, Prof A. de Smith, when drafting the Constitution for independent Mauritius drew inspiration from the European Convention, which exists since 1950, for the drafting of the

2

provisions relating to the protection of fundamental rights.

Now, the almost identical wording of Section 12 and Article 10 has led the Courts in Mauritius to interpret Section 12 liberally and in the same line as the European Court of Human Rights has for Article 10. The fact that the European Court has consistently shown how liberal it is in the interpretation of Article 10 can only be noted here as the greatest opportunity for the enjoyment of freedom of expression in Mauritius. The Supreme Court of Mauritius has admittedly not had the same opportunities as the European Court to examine the wording of these two articles and the principles applicable thereto but given the trend adopted by the Supreme Court of Mauritius to allow itself to be persuaded by the pronouncements of the European Court, I make it again plain that this in itself is the greatest opportunity not only for the media industry in Mauritius but for any citizen of this country.

Having said so, it is important now therefore to see how the European Court has interpreted the provisions of Article 10 so that one may gauge the ambit of Section 12 in Mauritius. From a reading of the recent pronouncement of the Grand Chamber of the European Court in the case of *Sanoma vs The Netherlands*, the following principles can be extracted:

Freedom of expression constitutes one of the essential foundations of a democratic society and the safeguards to be afforded to the press are of particular importance. Whilst the press must not overstep the bounds set, not only does the press have the task of imparting such information and ideas: the public also has a right to receive them. Were it otherwise, the press would be unable to play its vital role of "public watchdog" (Observer *and* Guardian *v. the United Kingdom*, 26 November 1991, § 59, Series A no. 216) The right of journalists to protect their sources is part of the freedom to "receive and impart information and ideas without interference by public authorities" protected by Article 10 of the Convention and serves as one of its important safeguards. It is a cornerstone of freedom of the press, without which sources may be deterred from assisting the press in informing the public on matters of public

3

interest. As a result the vital public-watchdog role of the press may be undermined and the ability of the press to provide accurate and reliable information to the public may be adversely affected.

The Court has always subjected the safeguards for respect of freedom of expression in cases under Article 10 of the Convention to special scrutiny. Having regard to the importance of the protection of journalistic sources for press freedom in a democratic society, an interference cannot be compatible with Article 10 of the Convention unless it is justified by an overriding requirement in the public interest (*Goodwin v. the United Kingdom*; *Roemen and Schmit v. Luxembourg*, no. 51772/99, ECHR 2003-IV; *Voskuil v. the Netherlands*,).

In *Goodwin v. the United Kingdom*, cited above, the Court held a disclosure order requiring a journalist to reveal the identity of a person who had provided him with information on an unattributable basis, and the fine imposed upon him for having refused to do so, to constitute an interference with the applicant's right to freedom of expression as guaranteed by paragraph 1 of Article 10.

In the *British Broadcasting Corporation* decision, the Commission distinguished the case of *Goodwin v. the United Kingdom* case on the grounds that Mr Goodwin had received information on a confidential and unattributable basis, whereas the information which the BBC had obtained comprised recordings of events that had taken place in public and to which no particular secrecy or duty of confidentiality could possibly attach." The Court notes that notwithstanding this finding the Commission "assume[d] an interference with the BBC's Article 10 rights in the case."

In *Roemen and Schmit v. Luxembourg*; *Ernst and Others v. Belgium*, no.33400/96, § 94, 15 July 2003; and again in *Tillack v. Belgium*, no.20477/05, § 56, ECHR 2007-XIII, the Court found that searches of journalists' homes and workplaces seeking to identify civil servants who had provided the journalists with confidential information constituted interferences with their rights guaranteed by paragraph 1 of Article 10. In *Roemen and Schmit, loc. cit.*, the Court also pointed out that the fact that the searches proved unproductive did not deprive them of their purpose, namely to establish the identity of the

4

journalist's source.

In *Voskuil v. the Netherlands*, an interference with the applicant's rights under Article 10 of the Convention was found in that a journalist's refusal to name the person who had presented him with information on alleged wrongdoing by police officers in a criminal investigation led the domestic court to order his detention in an attempt to compel him to speak.

Most recently, in *Financial Times Ltd and Others v. the United Kingdom*, no. 821/03, § 56, 15 December 2009, the Court found an order for the disclosure of the identity of an anonymous source of information addressed to four newspaper publishers and a news agency to constitute an interference with their rights under Article 10. Even though the order had not been enforced, that did not remove the harm to the applicant company since, however unlikely such a course of action might appear by the time the Court delivered its judgment, the order remained capable of being enforced.

On the facts of the case in Sanoma, the Grand Chamber concluded that the case concerned an order for the compulsory surrender of journalistic material which contained information capable of identifying journalistic sources. That in itself was sufficient for the Grand Chamber to find that this order constituted, in itself, an interference with the applicant company's freedom to receive and impart information under Article 10 § 1. The Grand Chamber also considered the question whether that order was "prescribed by law" as a permissible exception to Article 10 rights. The Grand Chamber considered that although there existed such a law, the quality of that law was deficient in that there was no procedure attended by adequate legal safeguards for the applicant company in order to enable an independent assessment as to whether the interest of the criminal investigation overrode the public interest in the protection of journalistic sources. There has accordingly been a violation of Article 10 of the Convention in that the interference complained of was not "prescribed by law." The Grand Chamber in the Sanoma case unanimously held that there had been a violation of Article 10 of the European Convention.

With this background, is it reassuring to recall that our final Court of Appeal is the Judicial Committee of the Privy Council? Whether the Judicial Committee is a constitutional anachronism or not is one matter. That it is our final court of appeal has always been and still is re-assuring in the circumstances especially for the protection of freedom of expression!

The next opportunity I wish to highlight is the independence of our Courts. We have seen how it is possible for a citizen to vindicate his freedom of expression by even seeking redress in the Courts. In the case of *Rogers vs. Controller of Customs*[2] in relation to a citizen's satellite dish (parabolic antenna) which was seized by the customs, the State had to bow down to the principles of freedom enshrined in our Constitution. In those days, i.e in the year 1990's, the use of parabolic antenna to receive signals from satellites was not authorised in Mauritius. Customs authorities purportedly abiding by customs regulations, refused to deliver that citizen's satellite dish at the time that it was being imported into Mauritius. That citizen seized the Supreme Court for an Order to release that satellite dish on the ground that he, as a citizen, was free to "receive" information and ideas without interference, and that the said customs laws, if any, restricted such enjoyment of the freedom of expression. The applicant in that case won the order of the day and took delivery of his parabolic antenna. The "telecommunications revolution" did not start with any government political will whatsoever; it was triggered by an ordinary citizen vindicating his constitutional right in the Courts. Following that decision in *Rogers*, the State had to enact the necessary legislation's to regulate broadcasting as well as the information and communication sectors. Private radios for instance thereupon came into existence. This opportunity of any citizen of vindicating his/her rights is the second most important opportunity I would highlight here.

Freedom of expression under Section 12 in Mauritius is enjoyed by all citizens. This means that the media and journalists enjoy no

---

[2] 1994 MR 144; see also judgment of the Appellate Court – 1994 SCJ 479

more or no less of such freedom. It follows that journalists require no form of licensing whatsoever to exercise their occupation as journalists. It is important to recognise that the State has not (yet) tried to subject journalists to any form of registration or licensing. This means that journalists enjoy this great opportunity to exercise their occupation within the ambit of the Constitution itself. The famous "Press Card" issued by the Government Information Service (GIS) of the Prime Minister's Office has too often been interpreted as a "license" or a "permit." It is not. It cannot in law be so. It is merely an identification document which the GIS issues to facilitate access of journalists to Government buildings for purposes of press conferences or such other purposes.

These being set down, it is now my invidious task to highlight some of the constraints, which, I am afraid, constitute the bulk of my paper.

These can be comprised into two: the legal constraints and the systemic constraints. Legal ones stem out of the legal system whilst the systemic ones stem of a culture of journalism which can and should be reformed.

The legal one – and it is really one major constraint – is unfortunately provided for by the Constitution itself: it is the restriction imposed upon public officers. Section 12 somehow strangely provides for a special restriction upon a special category of citizens known as "public officers." Section 12(2)(c) of the Constitution, as reproduced above, provides for this special restriction upon all "public officers."[3] The question whether such a restriction was designed during the aftermaths of the Second World War where any government information was confidential information, is indeed a subject for protracted debate. This is not the subject matter of this paper. Public Officers however are "silenced"!

---

[3] "public officer" means the holder of any public office and includes a person appointed to act in any public office; "public office" means, subject to section 112, an office of emolument in the public service; "public service" means the service of the State in a civil capacity in respect of the Government of Mauritius – see Section 111 of the Constitution of Mauritius.

This is the biggest constraint of the Mauritian citizen and more especially the Mauritian public officer and by extension the biggest constraint for the media. This not only hampers but altogether prevents the flow of information. The questions are: what if the information concerns an illegal act? What if the information concerns a potentially illegal act? Should the public officer remain in his "silence" until allowed to speak? How to strike the balance between the interests of a fundamental freedom of an individual and the "right" of a State to "secrecy"? The eminent human rights lawyers, Geoffrey Robertson QC and Andrew Nicol QC, say in their book "Media Law" in the opening paragraph of the chapter "Reporting Whitehall":

> *"Secrecy, said Richard Crossman, is the British disease. Government administrators catch it from the Official Secrets Act and supporting legislation. It is aggravated by bureaucratic rules and arrangements that conspire to place the United Kingdom toward the bottom in the league table of openness in Western democratic government. Against those who would hide their publicly paid behaviour from the public eye, the professional journalist can have only one response: to press on investigating and publishing, irrespective of the law. Most of the secrecy rules described in this chapter deserve to be broken, and many are, in fact, broken by the media regularly and without repercussions."*

The Mauritian civil servant suffers from that very same disease of "secrecy"! And the repeated reminders by way of the famous "circulars" lately that civil servants should not "speak to the press" indeed show that our civil servants are not likely to be relieved of this disease any time soon.

This state of affairs has as consequence that there is no free flow of information. Journalists have to battle against the numerous bureaucratic rules to obtain information and this indeed, in the words of Robertson and Nicol, place Mauritius toward the bottom of the league table of openness…

Now the disease of "secrecy" affecting civil servants is made worse. The next constraint to be highlighted in Mauritius is the quasi absence of a right to information. The absence of any Freedom of Information Act in Mauritius makes access to information a Herculean task. The citizen, or the journalist for that matter, has no legal means to obtain government information inasmuch as the legal system does not as yet recognise a "right to information." Successive governments, ever since 1995 up to date, have repeatedly and publicly announced their intention to enact such legislation but it does not look like this will become reality in the near future. The absence of such a legislation is simply incomprehensible and is a major constraint for the media industry. Citizens have the limited recourse of perhaps convincing their elected members of the National Assembly to be kind enough to address a Parliamentary Question to the relevant Minister so that the latter may answer and thereby provide the required information but that can admittedly only be done on issues of national importance. Citizens, but more often journalists, are thus driven to adopt other "darker" avenues of obtaining information and this puts both the civil servant as well as that journalist in a position of vulnerability. Indeed while the civil servant exposes himself to disciplinary action and possibly even criminal sanctions when giving out government information, the journalist exposes himself as well as his media house to government reprisals or even criminal action as will be seen below.

The other constraint, but in no way lesser in importance, is the existence in our criminal law of the offence of criminal defamation. Criminal defamation is clearly a Damocles sword hanging over each and every journalist in our country and this creates a profound "chilling effect" on them while they exercise their occupation. In recent years we have seen in this country that the arrests of journalists are on the increase while prosecutions for the very same cases do not necessarily follow. Such arrests of journalists only deepen this "chilling effect" on journalists. The UK, if an example is to be cited, has recently recognised that such an offence as criminal defamation could not be allowed to stand in modern days. Indeed, the new UK law - The Coroners and Justice Act 2009 which received the Royal Assent on 12th November 2009 – brought sweeping changes to the infamous UK law on sedition and libel. What is interesting to note is the words of Lord Bach, Parliamentary Under Secretary of State contained in a "Report to the House of Lords" dated 14th October 2009 where he wrote the following:

Coroners and Justice Bill: Report stage amendments

I am writing to let you have details of the Government amendments for Report which I have tabled today.

Sedition and seditious, defamatory and obscene libel (New Clause 'Abolition of common law libel offences etc.', amendments to clauses 170 and 171 and to schedules 20 and 22)

These amendments respond to the commitments I gave at Committee Stage (Official Report, 9 July 2009, cols 850), in response to amendments tabled by Lord Lester, to bring forward Government amendments to abolish the common law offences of sedition and seditious and defamatory libel.

Lord Lester, Evan Harris (who tabled similar amendments in the Commons), English PEN, the Organisation for Security and Co-operation in Europe and others have argued that these common law offences are anachronistic and that the continuing existence of such laws in the United Kingdom, albeit seldom used, has been cited by other countries as justification for the retention of similar laws which have been actively used to restrict press freedom.

Having considered the representations from Evan Harris and various organisations we are satisfied that these offences can be abolished without further ado.

Following our examination of the detail of Evan Harris's amendments, we have concluded that as a corollary we can also abolish the offence of libel. Obscene libel is one of the four forms of criminal libel originally covered by the

10

common law. If seditious libel and defamatory libel are abolished, it will be the only form of libel that is criminal at common law. (Blasphemous libel was abolished by the Criminal Justice and Immigration Act 2008.) However, it has effectively been superseded by the Obscene Publications Act 1959, section 2(4) of which provides that a person who publishes an article shall not be proceeded against for an offence at common law consisting of the publication of any matter included in the article where the essence of the offence is that the matter is obscene. As the offence of obscene libel have been rendered nugatory by section 2(4) of the 1959 Act, the Government amendments abolish it alongside seditious and defamatory libel. The amendments also include a number of consequential amendments to and repeals of existing statutory provisions in respect of criminal libel.

The abolition of these offences will extend to England and Wales and to Northern Ireland. Any equivalent changes in Scotland would be a matter for the Scottish Parliament and Government; I understand that the Scottish Government is considering the issue.

Many of the elected representatives in this country find comfort in looking up to the UK for inspiration. It is hoped that they will indeed be inspired in this case and perhaps realise that, more often than not, criminal defamation laws serve as weapons in the hands of the powerful to limit criticism and to stifle public debate. Perhaps they will also realise that criminal defamation laws pose a threat of criminal sanctions – especially imprisonment – and that this exerts in turn a profound chilling effect on freedom of expression. The time has indeed come for Mauritius to review its anachronistic criminal offences such as sedition (section 283 etc. Criminal Code), criminal defamation (section 288 Criminal Code) and the like.

Concerning the "systemic constraints" one can list the following which stem from the local context in which the media operates:

(i)   the relative small size of the market for the media;
(ii)   government influence
(iii)   lack of training of journalists

The relative small size of the market in Mauritius where the total population is about 1.2 million inhabitants makes media actors prone to being influenced by factors extraneous to their control such as advertising which indeed includes government advertising. Small size of the market means smaller revenue from direct sales such that advertising shares a greater importance as compared to sales. Advertising is thus a major consideration in media houses. Publication of an article one way or the other can have direct consequences on advertising whether by way of reward or reprisals. This is equally true for private sector companies as well as government advertising. The figures for private sector companies are quite hard to compile but the recent figures published as a result of a parliamentary question reveal which media house obtained how much of government advertising in recent years and it is not difficult to relate one to the other!

Concerning the issue of training, it is my personal experience as a part-time lecturer in Media Law as well as a number of years of personal interaction with the press which leads me to say in no uncertain terms that our journalists are lacking in training as to where they stand in their occupation as "journalists." Lack of training for journalists as to their rights and responsibilities has as direct consequence that journalists become easily influenced whether by their "informer" or the "advertiser" or indeed the government official who threatens "reprisals." Had Mr Bill Goodwin in the UK been lacking as to his knowledge of where he stood, he would surely have given the information which the Courts in the UK were compelling him to reveal. But he did not and the European Court proved him right many years later[4]. Media industry need to train their staff and the reason for doing so is simple: to equip them to battle their way through the number of constraints that come in their way. Journalists indeed have to battle in our country. And this is so in other countries too. Geoffrey Robertson QC and Andrew Nicol QC have this to say in their book "Media Law":

---

[4] See judgment of the European Court in *Goodwin vs. UK*

12

"Our hope is that journalists and broadcasters and their lawyers will regard the book not merely as a manual for self-defence, but as a guide to a complicated armoury of legal weapons for battering down doors unnecessarily shut in their faces"

The importance of training of the directors of media houses should not be minimised. They after all run a business which is or can easily be influenced, as highlighted above, by external factors such as business or political concerns.

One final word for this paper: journalists and broadcasters do enjoy "rights." One should however never lose sight of the fact that others have valid claims to legal protection as well; such as the right to lead a private life free from media harassment and embarrassment[5] , to undergo a trial by an independent and impartial Court as opposed to a "trial by the press," and more especially to have false accusations corrected swiftly and with the same prominence as they are made. These issues, as well as the issue of whether there is a need for the setting up of a "Media Ombudsman" in Mauritius will however be discussed in another forum – perhaps a forthcoming dialogue!

---

[5] Article 22 Code Civil – Chacun a droit au respect de sa vie privée

Freedom and Transparency: A Journalistic Appreciation

Subash Gobine
Senior Editor at Defi Media Group

How is freedom defined in our trade? Is it absolute freedom to publish or broadcast? Or is freedom a matter of degree?

In fact, freedom is rather seen as a matter of degree. For it is always debatable whether we are fully free or partly free.

In Mauritius, the press enjoys freedom to the extent it is guaranteed by the Constitution of the land. That freedom is restrained, however, by provisions of the law regarding libel in civil law and so-called 'criminal defamation' as provided for in criminal law.

Freedom is also measured in terms of intervention from the State. Empirical evidence suggests that the State has been using a whole gamut of formal and informal measures to impress upon media practitioners to 'toe the line'.

For the past months, we have witnessed a trend towards using the police apparatus and the regulatory framework to rein in practitioners whose reports have challenged the political establishment. Reporters have actually been arrested for allegedly committing some type of misdemeanour on charges as fanciful as infringement on 'restricted' property. Charges of publishing false news have also been initiated in some cases.

Furthermore, politicians in power have not failed to register complaints with the Independent Broadcasting Authority (IBA) following statements made or reports carried on private radios.

It often happens that charges are dropped but the end result of journalists facing prosecution, in government's expectation, is practitioners internalizing the need for greater caution in delivering news or expressing viewpoints, if not practising outright self-censorship.

The psychological pressure on private radios is still stronger as their functions and obligations are well defined in the law. The policy maker can revoke a broadcast licence or choose not to renew it.

Government can also use other institutions to restrict press freedom. Empirical evidence shows that the tax department, the pension office and the labour inspectorate have been used to harass newspaper companies. Private companies having the State as controlling shareholder can serve as a bargaining chip in business dealings with private media. The advertising budget of such State-controlled companies can also be used as leverage in case of conflict between the government and media.

The advertising resources of State institutions have for long been used as a strategic weapon by each successive Government engaged in a sanctions/reward game with the media. One media house is presently suing the State on this issue, its contention being arbitrary boycott in government advertising in spite of its purported wide audience.

Understandably, pro-government media are handsomely rewarded with government advertising funds, whatever be their circulation or audience. Advertising revenue is denied or restricted in volume to media suspected of being hostile to government.

Depriving newspapers of advertising revenue has developed into a natural reflex among partisan strategists. One particular case in point goes back to the early seventies. A pro-Government lobby called Le Club des Coalisés Réalistes, was close to Gaëtan Duval, leader of the Parti Mauricien Social Democrate (PMSD). Duval, a fiery Opposition figure, had joined Sir Seewoosagur Ramgoolam in a government coalition. The PMSD lobby brought pressure to build on *Le Mauricien* daily and the *Week-End* weekly. The two papers were accused of supporting the new Opposition force, the Mouvement

16

Militant Mauricien (MMM). This pressure group impressed upon private companies not to provide advertising revenue to *Le Mauricien* and *Week-End*. The editors of the newspapers were also subjected to moral harassment. One editor was actually forced into exile.

Moral harassment has often been deployed by government leaders to destabilize editors or senior journalists perceived as being supportive of the Opposition. Following the general election of 1983 when the MMM made a bid for power, the chief editors of two dailies having the largest circulation were systematically harassed by government parties to the point that both retired after the MMM lost the election. Names of targeted journalists suspected of supporting the MMM were mentioned during mass rallies when supporters were whipped into a frenzy.

Such harassment is also meant to drive home to shareholders of media companies the threat of financial boycott or hostile State intervention in their own business dealings. As the cover price of a newspaper hardly meets the cost of production, media executives rely heavily on advertising to stay in business. The cost of importing newsprint from distant suppliers weighs heavily on the operating expenses of newspapers. The prospect of losing Government advertising and the threat of private sector advertising revenue being compromised are likely to deter newspaper companies from supporting a senior journalist. In a cost-benefit analysis, editorial independence is outweighed by economics.

Still, in restraining press freedom, even more potent than outright financial strangulation or moral harassment stands the formidable weapon of libel. In the Mauritian environment, libel laws are heavily loaded in favour of parties taking exception to a press report which is written in good faith, in the public interest but not totally accurate. It is often a difficult task to prove the accuracy of such a report in the absence of official documents. Indeed, access to official documents is denied under the provisions of the Official Secrets Act. No State employee will be willing to depone in favour of the media in a libel case.

Where the good faith of the media would be upheld in Western courts of law, such cases are likely to fail in Mauritius if the materiality of the facts mentioned in an article is not proven. Good faith and the public interest do not always prevail in Mauritius.

By filing a series of lawsuits based on fine legal points, a political lobby stands a good chance of destabilising the personnel of a newspaper whose representatives will have to spend considerable time attending court proceedings. A daily supporting an opposition party folded in the past after it failed to meet the cost of libel damage.

As of late, a rarely used legal provision - that of criminal defamation - is being increasingly used against the media. The law provides for the arrest and prosecution of any practitioner or publisher following a complaint made to the police by an aggrieved party. Since criminal defamation is an arrestable offence, any journalist facing such a charge has to go through the technical process of going under police custody before being released on bail. The provision of criminal defamation has been removed from the statute books of England. But, Mauritius is following a contrary trend.

Initiating libel cases in civil courts and criminal defamation proceedings forms part of a strategy to instil a reflex of self-censorship among media practitioners. Once cases are brought before the court, newspapers would tend to refrain from writing on the issue to avoid the risk of committing the offence of contempt of the court. It is not a rare occurrence in Mauritius to use some form of legal gagging to stop a public scandal from causing further damage.

Besides soft tactics of economic boycott and legal pressure, the provision of 'trespassing' has been used against two reporters who went to investigate a case of neighbourhood noise level complaint opposing a group of residents and a political bigwig. A similar argument of trespassing was also used against two radio reporters who were investigating a case against a cleric. They were even beaten up in a place of worship by the supporters of the cleric.

Freedom of the press is also restrained in Mauritius by the absence of competition in free-to-air broadcast television. A partial liberalisation of the electronic media was carried out in 2001 and three private radios were licensed to operate. However, the government of the day failed to keep its electoral promise of privatising one of the three analogue television channels of the public broadcaster. All governments in Mauritius invariably use public television as an effective communication tool. Surveys prove that public television has a wide viewership. It is also believed that in the course of the last electoral campaign, government spin doctors extensively used television to undermine the Opposition. Though the enactment on the public broadcaster prohibits partisan bias, the Opposition did not make a legal challenge in Court on that issue.

Free-to-air television is available in almost all households in Mauritius. Satellite television providing content from abroad is allowed in Mauritius. However, satellite television accessibility is limited as households already pay a fee of Rs. 100 (around $3) per month to the public broadcaster. They are reticent to pay about ten times more to access foreign channels that do not provide local content, still less political news and reports on the Mauritian setup. By migrating to digital technology, the public broadcaster has developed capacity to run as many as sixteen channels now. Government has so far not shown its willingness to make available the least television channel to a private company. By running several channels, the public broadcaster has created the impression that diversity exists while it is more than obvious that state monopoly stays entrenched. It is also pre- empting competition by crowding the market.

Technological innovation may still allow some form of private IPTV but again, accessibility to computers is not as universal as television. IPTV would hardly match the reach and firepower of the public free-to-air broadcasts.

Freedom of the press in Mauritius is inextricably linked to the issue of transparency. What is behind the delivery of news in the media? Who owns the media? And is there a particular agenda each media outlet is serving? The answer to these questions will help shed light on how transparent the media of Mauritius are.

It is obvious in the case of the public broadcaster that the State enjoys a monopoly on free-to-air television. The State effectively controls both the Board of the Mauritius Broadcasting Corporation and its management. Indeed, the Prime Minister appoints the director-general of the MBC. In at least three cases, the director-general served as adviser at the Prime Minister's Office before being appointed as head of the public broadcasting corporation. The first ever director-general was a former member of the legislative team of the Labour party. The close links between the head of government and the head of the MBC have been instrumental in shaping the policy of the public broadcaster and in its modus operandi as a key instrument in delivering government and party-in-power communication.

The partisan control of the MBC has long stayed a major controversy in Mauritius. Opposition parties always undertake to free the MBC from political control. However, once in power, all parties come to realise that considerable benefits in terms of almost universal communication could be derived from controlling the public broadcaster.

When three private radio licences were issued, new actors emerged in the business of electronic media. Two of the three private radios were linked to two newspaper companies that eventually developed into the two leading media houses of Mauritius. The third radio was associated with a foreign operator already running such a business in England. While the third radio chose not to upset the government, the two radio stations associated with newspaper companies made it a point to sharpen their differences with the public radio broadcaster by adopting an aggressive anti-Establishment line. Understandably, the ownership of the two radio stations and suspicions of their partisan bias - a matter of controversy - became a political issue. The two stations very quickly won a big audience, overtaking all public channels.

To better understand how transparency is linked to ownership and how control of the media becomes an issue of politics, economic power and ethnicity in a plural society like Mauritius, reference will have to be made to some historical facts. Ever since French colonisation and well until the

1850s, that is 40 years after British rule, the print media were owned by the French Whites who controlled the economy. In fact, the longest French White-owned newspaper, *Le Cernéen*, was launched in a context where slavery was being abolished in the British Empire. French White slave- owning planters launched *Le Cernéen* to fight for their financial interests. The paper survived as a mouthpiece for the economic and political rights of French Whites well into the late 1970s.

As from the 1950s, a new class of Mauritians came to be involved in newspaper publishing. Indeed, the community known as the Coloured made of people of mixed European, African and Indian origin came to assert its rights in opposition to the White oligarchy. The man fighting for this cause, Rémy Ollier, published the first non-White paper called *La Sentinelle*. Though *La Sentinelle* did not stay long in business, a new phenomenon came to be established in the media landscape - the ability of the Coloured to play a decisive role in shaping public opinion.

Ever since Ollier, Coloured ownership of the media helped to a large extent in legitimising the rights of this community in colonial times. The term Coloured was later abandoned and the Creole label came to be increasingly used. In the 1920s, a Creole family took control of a White-owned paper, *Le Mauricien*.

Later, when accession to independence opposed the Labour Party and the PMSD, White and Creole papers played a key role in supporting the White- sponsored PMSD in opposing the end of colonial rule. In fact, in the face of what was perceived as a threat of Hindu hegemony following independence, the French White economic establishment and Coloured lobbies combined their efforts in fighting the Hindu-supported Labour Party. The PMSD managed to rally almost all non-Hindu votes against the Labour Party.

Not all Creole papers supported the PMSD. In fact, a group of pro-Labour Creole professionals and intellectuals started a paper, *L'express*, in 1963. The main objective of *L'express* was to respond to the highly effective impact *Le Mauricien* and *Le Cernéen* were having on the non-Hindu component of the population. But in a matter of time, *L'express* chose to rebrand itself as mainstream paper and adopted techniques of professional journalism. The paper is strongly supported by the business community. The family owning *Le Mauricien* later launched a very successful Sunday paper, *Week-End*. That media house has changed policy after independence, by branding itself as a mainstream paper. *Le Cernéen* collapsed in the late 1970s.

Still on the issue of ownership of media and transparency, though some marginal 'Indian' newspapers came to be published in the early 1900s, it was not until the early 1940s that the first 'Indian' owned French-language daily came to join the debate. That paper, *Advance*, was launched by Muslim traders and Hindu intellectuals. In a matter of time, it became the most popular daily of the country. But its influence declined after independence. It actually folded after the Labour Party suffered its first- ever electoral defeat in 1982. A Muslim-owned pro-Labour daily, *The Star*, became a weekly and has survived so far. Other Hindu-owned French- language papers, *The Nation* (pro-Labour) and *The Sun* supporting the Mouvement Socialiste Militant (MSM) of the Jugnauth family have not managed to survive beyond two decades.

Ownership of the print media has been largely in Creole hands. Those papers have claimed a wide readership in all communities. By commanding such an extensive reach in the population, Creole papers have been challenged by the Hindu political elite which suspects those media outlets of supporting the Opposition. When the MMM challenged Aneerood Jugnauth in 1983 and fielded Paul Bérenger as a contender for Prime- ministership, an acrimonious debate started on the role of *Le Mauricien* and *L'express* in determining the outcome of the election. Jugnauth's party and its Labour and PMSD allies openly attacked the two papers. After they won the election, the editors of the two papers were removed by their respective companies.

The Hindu political establishment often expresses its nervousness in the face of its inability to control the print media and the privately-owned radio stations.

Since the late 1980s, the country is witnessing a paradigm shift in media ownership. The readership of the Creole-owned print media has faced constant erosion after the arrival of new players, mainly the Defi Media house which runs a daily, two weeklies and the most popular radio platform, Radio Plus. A new daily, *Le Matinal*, has also built readership at the expense of Creole-owned papers. Radio One which forms part of the *L'express* media house is outgunned by Radio Plus and the combination of all public radios.

The new media landscape of the 21st century will probably see an accelerated diversification of ownership. Empirical evidence suggests the Hindu political elite and Muslim business and political interests seem to be mounting a challenge to French-White control of the economy. As control of the print and electronic media has been linked in the past to the capture - or denial of - political power, it is more than likely that ownership and transparency will fuel public debate for quite some time in the future. The Hindu political elite is unlikely to relinquish control of public broadcasting while it is determined to restrict the reach of a section of the print media. Only time will tell if it will be a total war between political power and the platforms of mass communication (print, electronic, Internet). Or, whether it will be a limited war between power and the traditional print media.

3

Freedom and Transparency: A Journalistic Appreciation

Gilbert Ahnee
Editor-in-Chief at La Sentinelle

When one lives in a democracy, knowing that the Rule of Law is effective enough to protect anyone from being arbitrarily arrested and sent to jail, when one is free to voice out one's opinions and lambast the Prime Minister or the Leader of the Opposition, one should be cautious before describing that dispensation as a dictatorship. Right from the outset, I wish to say that Mauritius is not a dictatorship, I wish to add that the press in this country enjoys freedoms – freedom from invasive political influence as well as freedom from indiscreet financial stake holding – liberties of action and operation which many peers, in Europe or the US, can envy us.

Let it be put on record: Mauritius is not a dictatorship, journalism is exercised in a largely free environment. So far, so good. But can it be enough? Probably not.

Journalists have been accused, over the last months, of publishing false material or, at least, incomplete or slanted reports. I shall refrain from saying that these accusations provide an accurate description of the situation but I cannot, either, shy away from the glaring reality that many stories carried in our papers fall short of the standards expected from quality publications. Are the papers, or the journalists or their editors responsible for that? Not at all in most cases, not totally in some others. This presentation is supposed to address the issue of transparency and, at least as regards stories about questions of public governance, the lack of transparency, the culture of retention of information are at the very heart of the problem.

I fully agree that, quite often, journalists don't even care to seek the other side of the story in view of a balanced report. In a high-profiled case of the previous decade, I have had, personally, in my editorial capacity, to deal with a so-called seasoned journalist who claimed that his sources were official – police sources, as a matter of fact – and that there was no need to provide a better deal, a fair deal, to the accused person. I still support the view that, at least through the latter's lawyer, his version of the story was needed.

But we were talking about official sources and the culture of retention of information. We still operate in Mauritius, under what I will call the "legal trauma" of the Official Secrets Act. If journalists in my position are prepared to accept that their profession has not always been beyond reproach, other stakeholders in the information process should also admit that they also have a share of responsibility towards improving the overall quality of news reporting.

En passant: Journalists should be cautious vis-à-vis the apparently modern "openness" of sources in the business milieu. They appear in sharp contrast with the opacity of government and administration but communication is not information. Coming to the latter, coming to the information we need from official sources, turning the page of the Official Secrets Act would mean, at long last, adopting a Freedom of Information Act.

It is worth here recalling that, at the 11th Commonwealth Law Ministers Meeting in May 1999, the following resolutions were adopted:

• Member countries should be encouraged to regard Freedom of Information as a legal and enforceable right;

• There should be a presumption in favour of disclosure and governments should promote a culture of openness;

• The right of access to information may be subject to limited exemptions, but these should be drawn narrowly;

• Governments should maintain and preserve records;

• In principle, decisions to refuse access to records and information should be subject to independent review.

However, eleven years have elapsed. Nothing has really been done to turn these resolutions to reality...

4

Élargir l'Espace Démocratique: La presse mauricienne et le citoyen informé

Catherine Boudet
Docteur en Sciences Politiques et Journaliste

Un consensus existe, parmi les journalistes comme parmi les sociologues des médias, sur l'idée que la presse a un rôle à jouer dans l'élargissement de l'espace démocratique. Ce rôle de «facilitateur de citoyenneté» dont serait doté la presse procèderait de sa capacité à fournir aux lecteurs l'accès à l'information nécessaire et indispensable pour l'exercice de citoyenneté. Ce postulat repose largement sur la théorie fondatrice du philosophe allemand Jürgen Habermas sur l'espace public[6] , en vertu de laquelle l'accès à l'information permet aux citoyens d'être «éclairés», c'est-à-dire d'avoir la capacité à débattre des affaires publiques.

Néanmoins, pour le lecteur-citoyen, être « bien informé » ne signifie pas seulement recevoir de l'information en vrac. Il lui faut aussi savoir comment la trier et quoi en faire, afin d'être en mesure d'y porter un regard critique afin de pouvoir débattre des affaires de la Cité. A cet égard, il apparaît donc que la mission de la presse d'information du citoyen ne s'arrête pas au rôle de fournisseur d'information, mais s'accompagne donc aussi de la responsabilité de fournir à ce dernier les moyens d'appréhender cette information de façon constructive et responsable. Il s'agit, comme le soulignait Waheed Khan, assistant directeur général pour l'Information et la Communication à l'UNESCO, de pourvoir les citoyens des *«instruments nécessaires pour opérer des choix informés et accroître leur*

---

[6] Jürgen Habermas, *The Structural Transformation of the Public Sphere*, publié en allemand en 1962.

participation à la prise de décision sur des sujets qui affectent leur existence."[7]

La condition d'existence d'un espace public réside dans «*la présence de médias susceptibles d'alimenter et d'éclairer le débat public*»[8], rappelle le sociologue américain, spécialiste des médias, Michael Schudson. L'espace public c'est en effet, suivant Jürgen Habermas, cet espace symbolique, interface entre la société et l'État, où peuvent se débattre les affaires publiques, sur la base d'une critique raisonnée.

La notion d'espace public implique donc deux éléments essentiels: d'une part, l'importance de l'opinion publique, c'est-à-dire d'une aptitude et d'une légitimité des citoyens à exprimer un jugement critique du pouvoir politique. D'autre part, la notion de «*publicité critique*," terme forgé par le philosophe allemand pour signifier qu'il est impératif, pour que se forme cette opinion publique, de disposer de l'information sur le fonctionnement de l'État. Habermas pose de cette façon la constitution d'un espace public comme condition d'une compétence politique et d'un exercice de la citoyenneté. Et c'est donc grâce à la médiation des organes de presse que l'autorité publique peut être soumise au tribunal d'une critique rationnelle et légitime.

Or, le rôle de la presse dans cette « publicité critique », est loin d'être neutre. D'abord, parce que, comme le souligne Michael Schudson, elle place l'information « *au centre d'un forum où elle peut être discutée par l'ensemble de la population* »4 , ce qui a pour effet de stimuler l'interaction entre les différentes composantes de la société. Ce faisant, la presse confère une légitimité, mais aussi une amplification à l'information qu'elle véhicule, note Michael Schudson5. Comme l'observe Henri Valot, professeur de philosophie politique, sur le site web Civicus, la presse joue un rôle de « *plage grise* ," à cheval entre le secteur privé et la société civile, plage grise « *essentielle au travail*

---

[7] Abdul Waheed Khan, Préface, *Media Development Indicators, a framework for assessing media development*, UNESCO, 26ème session de l'Interdevelopment Council of the International Programme for the Development of Communication (IPDC), 26-28 mars 2008.

[8] Michael Schudson, *Le pouvoir des médias, Journalisme et démocratie*, Paris, Nouveaux horizons, 1995, p. 241.

contemporain de plaidoyer, car ainsi la société civile et les organisations qui la représentent sont prises au sérieux, mais aussi questionnées, par la presse qui leur offre un espace »[9] Quant à Pierre Bourdieu, il concevait même le journalisme comme un service public à part entière.[10]

Il ressort donc que le rôle de la presse dans l'élaboration d'un espace public ne s'arrête pas à délivrer de l'information. Ce faisant, la presse contribue à façonner des cadres de pensée : *« La presse contribue à l'élaboration du contexte dans lequel et à partir duquel se forme la pensée du citoyen »*[11].

Du point de vue du lecteur, il ne suffit pas d'avoir accès à l'information pour être informé. Le citoyen «bien» informé, c'est celui qui bénéficie de l'information mais aussi de la hauteur de vue et des critères de jugement qui lui permettent de donner sens à ces éléments d'information reçus9. D'autant que l'information, ce n'est pas seulement cet ensemble de données sur ce qui se passe dans le monde alentour. L'information constitue bien un *« savoir collectif»*,10 en ce qu'elle s'élabore conjointement, par celui qui l'émet et par celui qui la reçoit, voire par la chaîne des intervenants entre ces deux pôles. Et si les cadres de pensée qui accompagnent cette information sont pauvres, c'est autant d'appauvrissement pour l'espace public et pour l'avancée du débat démocratique.

Si la presse veut se prévaloir d'un rôle dans la construction de la citoyenneté, il lui est nécessaire aussi d'examiner son rôle dans la construction des savoirs collectifs.[12] Or, il apparaît qu'à Maurice, cette

---

[9] Henri Valot, « Organisations de la société civile et médias : une alliance tacite ?," CIVICUS World Alliance of Citizen Participation, http://www.civicus.org/desk-of-secretary-general/french-version/1088-organisations-de-la-societe-civile-et-medias--une-alliance-tacite-.

[10] Pierre Bourdieu, «Journalisme et éthique», *Les cahiers du journalisme*, juin 1996, n°1.

[11] Michael Schudson, *op. cit.,* p. 22.

[12] La notion de « construction des savoirs » vient du psychologue français Jean Piaget, pour qui l'apprentissage se réalise dans l'interaction entre l'individu et son environnement. La notion de cadre social est donc déterminante dans l'acquisition de connaissances et dans leur transformation en apprentissage. Car ce cadre social fournit en grande partie les bases du sens sur lesquelles va reposer la construction des savoirs, alors que l'individu produit dans l'apprentissage ses

construction des savoirs collectifs est fortement carencée.

Les carences du dialogue démocratique mauricien

A Maurice, l'exercice de production de ce « *savoir collectif* » qu'est l'information, est sévèrement contraint par un ensemble de facteurs en premier lieu institutionnels. Ceux-ci tiennent en particulier à la difficulté d'autonomisation de l'espace public vis-à-vis du politique.

Dans le système politique mauricien d'essence westminstérienne, c'est le Parlement qui est considéré comme le seul légitime pour assurer la transmission des revendications sociales vers l'État[13]. C'est donc seulement par le biais de ses députés, à travers les questions parlementaires, que le citoyen peut espérer demander des comptes au gouvernement.

L'État mauricien exerce même une certaine forme de *containment* à l'encontre des expressions de la société civile. Cette politique de *containment* s'exprime principalement par un arsenal juridique, notamment les législations répressives sur le droit de grève ou de manifestation (*Industrial Relations Act* ou *Public Gathering Act*), auxquelles vient s'ajouter l'absence d'un *Freedom of Information Act*.

Cette politique de *containment* a des raisons historiques, puisqu'elle est liée à la mise en place d'un modèle de démocratie d'essence «consociative," c'est-à-dire un *power sharing* entre élites supposées représenter les différents groupes ethniques.[14] Or, ces ententes au sommet entre élites, ont besoin, pour fonctionner, d'une certaine opacité vis-à-vis de la société civile.[15]

---

propres règles et modèles mentaux.

[13] Catherine Boudet, «Société civile et politique : le dialogue de sourds," *Impact* n°5 du 09 avril 2010.

[14] Catherine Boudet, « L'émergence de la démocratie consociative à Maurice (1948-1968) », *Annuaire des Pays de l'Océan Indien* n°17, 2003, pp. 325-336.

[15] « *La période de 1955 à 1967 a été celle des conférences constitutionnelles, qui ont réuni les élites politiques pour négocier une formule constitutionnelle. Celles-ci doivent alors mener simultanément les deux niveaux du jeu politique, la compétition dans l'arène électorale et la coopération au sommet de l'État. La règle du secret devient alors essentielle. Un exemple de cette pratique est celui des négociations secrètes qui ont entouré l'excision des Chagos* ». Catherine

L'interventionnisme de l'État, avait souligné Jürgen Habermas, dépossède l'espace public de ses fonctions critiques. On risque alors de voir s'installer un espace public purement acclamatif (inféodé au pouvoir politique), où le marketing politique se substitue à la discussion. C'est exactement ce qui se passe en contexte mauricien, où le débat démocratique est remplacé par du marketing politique.[16]

La presse mauricienne a donc une responsabilité accrue dans la mesure où, dans la démocratie mauricienne d'essence consociative, elle reste la seule sphère alternative au Parlement d'expression des demandes citoyennes envers l'État. Pourtant, à ces carences du dialogue démocratique, s'ajoute le constat, venant d'observateurs de la société civile, que la presse ne jouerait pas son rôle d'interface entre social et politique.

Les griefs des lecteurs envers la presse mauricienne

La presse mauricienne faillirait, déplorent ces observateurs, à relayer les débats sociaux, voire même à apporter des analyses objectives des faits de société et des questions politiques. C'est ce qui ressortait d'un article que nous avons écrit dans *Impact magazine* en mai 2010, «Presse et démocratie : un accommodement de surface».[17]

Ainsi, Nita Deerpalsing, responsable de la communication au Parti Travailliste, observe qu'«*il y a beaucoup de débats dans ce pays, peut-être que ce n'est pas répercuté au niveau des médias*». De l'avis de Lindsey Collen, dirigeante du parti *Lalit*, la couverture médiatique « *ne joue pas son rôle pour faire connaître la teneur de ces débats* ». Le syndicaliste Reeaz

---

Boudet, « Information : le droit de savoir », *l'express* du 04 septembre 2009.

[16] « *Le dialogue démocratique est remplacé par la "comm" politique : "On vend un produit, c'est-à-dire un parti et ses candidats," s'indigne Joceline Minerve. "Mais est-ce que les gens ont leur mot à dire sur le 24/7, sur la peine de mort? Les sujets sont mis à l'agenda politique du fait du caprice du Prince ou des partis. Voit-on les différents courants politiques traditionnels venir s'engager sur ces questions ?" Tout se passe comme si le système politique bloquait toute remontée de questions sociales qui ne seraient pas canalisées par l'espace parlementaire .*" Catherine Boudet, « *Société civile et politique : le dialogue de sourds,*" *Impact* n°5 du 09 avril 2010.

[17] Catherine Boudet, « Presse et démocratie : un accomodement de surface ," *Impact* n°9 du 07 mai 2010.

Chuttoo, dirigeant de la Confédération des Travailleurs du Secteur Privé (CTSP), note qu'il n'y a a « *pas beaucoup d'analyse objective* » dans la presse. Quant à Christina Chan-Meetoo, chargée de cours en communication à l'Université de Maurice, elle déplore que dans la presse mauricienne, généralement, « *même si on a les informations, on ne fait pas le croisement des données* ».

Un autre grief fait à la presse mauricienne par le lectorat est sa préférence pour une amplification de réactions d'ordre « communal » au détriment du débat d'idées. Certains lecteurs regrettent également une tendance à exagérer ou même à créer artificiellement des clivages. Ce qui, d'après Lindsey Collen, réduit le compte rendu de la politique à des batailles de clans, ou des affrontements. « *Ce faisant, les médias exacerbent la conscience communaliste au niveau de la population* ," observe un autre dirigeant de *Lalit,* Ram Seegobin.

En renforçant ainsi les travers de la population, la presse mauricienne ne joue pas son rôle de consolidation d'un espace public neutre et critique. Cette observation va dans le sens de la mise en garde qu'effectuait le *Media Development Indicators* de l'UNESCO, selon lequel « (…) *les médias peuvent parfois servir à asseoir des intérêts personnels et aggraver les inégalités sociales, en excluant les opinions critiques et marginalisées. Les médias peuvent même encourager le conflit et la discorde sociale* ».[18].

Ce faisant, la presse contribue même à entretenir certains blocages dans la société. Des blocages sociaux qui résultent déjà d'une difficulté à s'autonomiser vis-à-vis d'un modèle d'administration hérité de la colonisation britannique. « *On a un vrai problème de construction des savoirs à Maurice* », reconnaît Belall Maudarbux, enseignant-chercheur.

« *Notre modèle de savoir a toujours été un modèle par* copy-paste ."[19]. Une entrepreneure sociale, pionnière dans ce domaine à Maurice, Nathalia Vadamootoo, constatait elle aussi ce «*formatage dû à l'héritage*

[18] *Media Development Indicators, a framework for assessing media development, op. cit.,* Introduction, p. 3.
[19] Catherine Boudet, « Construction des savoirs à Maurice : Une démocratisation nécessaire ," *Impact* n°31 du 8 octobre 2010.

du modèle administratif britannique».[20]. Pour le linguiste Rada Tirvassen, la construction des savoirs à Maurice n'est pas centrée sur la formation du citoyen, mais sur la préparation des acteurs de la vie économique : « *On n'est pas dans un processus de construction des savoirs, mais dans un processus de construction des acteurs de l'économie* »[21]. C'est vrai pour l'éducation, mais c'est également vrai pour les médias, pourtant supposée prendre le relais de l'école, d'après Rada Tirvassen, qui constate « *une perte du regard critique dans les médias* »[22].

Nathalia Vadamootoo préconisait donc la nécessité de « *revisiter* » le modèle dont Maurice a hérité, ce qui nécessitera « *beaucoup de travail de recherche mais aussi de concertation entre les différentes parties de la société civile et de l'appareil public et du gouvernement* »[23]. Il apparaît justement qu'avec les nouvelles plateformes journalistiques que fournissent internet, blogs et forums virtuels notamment, se mettent en place les conditions technologiques de l'ouverture et de l'innovation sociale.

L'ouverture technologique pour favoriser l'innovation sociale

Il semble important, voire même urgent, de restaurer le rôle du journaliste dans la construction des savoirs collectifs. Ce qui ne veut pas dire que le journaliste doive usurper le rôle du pédagogue ou de l'universitaire. Mais il apparaît que le journalisme mauricien se retrouve dans la nécessité d'innover dans ses pratiques, s'il veut contribuer à « *empower* » le citoyen- lecteur. L'innovation sociale peut se définir comme une *«réponse nouvelle»* à un besoin social ou à une situation sociale jugée insatisfaisante. Elle constitue un dispositif d'accompagnement destiné à permettre d'*empower* l'individu, c'est-à-dire à lui permettre d'acquérir un développement personnel de façon à ce qu'il reprenne le pouvoir sur le déroulement de sa propre vie, c'est-à-dire à acquérir l'autonomie lui permettant de réorganiser son

---

[20] Catherine Boudet, « Natalia Vadamootoo introduit l'entreprise sociale à Maurice ," *Impact* n°20 du 23 juillet 2010.
[21] « Construction des savoirs à Maurice : Une démocratisation nécessaire ," *op. cit.*
[22] Ibid.
[23] « Natalia Vadamootoo introduit l'entreprise sociale à Maurice ," *op. cit.*

existence. L'innovation vise donc à mieux satisfaire «*les besoins non ou mal satisfaits par les moyens "officiels"*»[24]23 .

A l'heure de *Wikileaks* et des médias électroniques, l'innovation technologique apparaît comme un facteur d'entraînement pour l'innovation sociale, mais le processus est loin d'être mécanique ou évident. Certes, les médias électroniques peuvent constituer des « *outils de transformation de la société civile* »[25]24 , par le fait qu'ils créent des forums virtuels où chacun peut exprimer ses opinions ou manifester son opposition. Philip N. Howard, professeur en Communication à l'Université de Washington, note à cet égard qu'ils jouent ainsi un rôle essentiel de « *protection de la gestation du discours politique* »[26]25 , en particulier dans les contextes où il existe des risques de censure.

Néanmoins, les métiers de la presse doivent déjà appréhender ces innovations technologiques et leurs implications, avant de se prétendre porteurs d'une innovation sociale. La transformation de l'espace public apportée par les médias électroniques implique en premier chef la fin de la séparation traditionnelle entre professionnels et amateurs, entre spécialistes et amateurs, dans la mesure où «*l'Internet a ouvert un espace pour des formes d'expertises publiques portées par des individus ou des collectifs de tous ordres* »[27] . Un nouveau modèle éditorial se fait jour, dans lequel le contrôle de la qualité de l'information aussi change : « *Le contrôle de la qualité de l'information n'est pas réalisé a priori par un système de sélection éditorial pyramidal et certifié mais par un contrôle a posteriori dans lequel la qualité des informations est principalement une conséquence du travail des lecteurs* »[28] .

De sorte que le journaliste peut se retrouver de plus en plus

---

[24] Julie Cloutier, « Qu'est-ce que l'innovation sociale ? ," *Etudes théoriques*, n°ET0314, Centre de recherches sur les innovations sociales, Université de Québec, Montréal, novembre 2003, p. 41.
[25] Philip N. Howard, « Les médias électroniques, outils de transformation de la société civile», http://www.america.gov/st/democracyhr-french/2010/January/20100226105922mlenuhret0.8975489.html
[26] Ibid.
[27] Dominique Cardon, « La blogosphère est-elle un espace public comme les autres?," *Transversales Sciences & Culture*, 26 avril 2006, http://grit-transversales.org/article.php3?id_article=100
[28] Ibid.

exposé à la critique ou à la remise en question par son lectorat. Ceci peut être vécu comme une fragilisation par ce dernier. Mais cet « *élargissement du cercle des preneurs de parole* » grâce à Internet et l'inter-régulation qui se met en place sont le signe d'un exercice de la citoyenneté, par l'exercice d'un « *travail collectif de mise en débat d'argumentation* », rappelle Dominique Cardon.[29]

Michael Schudson identifie les fonctions nécessaires que les médias devraient remplir afin de mieux servir la démocratie, c'est-à-dire pour permettre à chacun de prendre en tout connaissance de cause les décisions qui lui incombent en tant que citoyen : offrir une information impartiale et complète ; offrir un cadre cohérent pour aider les citoyens à comprendre le monde politique; être les « *transporteurs publics* » servant à véhiculer les différents points de vue de la société; et enfin, offrir un forum où les citoyens peuvent dialoguer.[30]

A Maurice, on parle couramment de *Corporate Social Responsibility* (CSR) des entreprises, cette responsabilité sociale des entreprises qui est d'apporter une aide aux projets de développement sociaux. Il apparaît que la presse aussi a sa propre « Responsabilité Sociale »[31] Le lecteur mauricien le dit souvent : il est las des éditoriaux ou des articles « à agenda » qui prétendent lui dicter ce qu'il doit faire et ce qu'il doit penser. Il veut pouvoir obtenir une information à partir de laquelle il pourra se forger sa propre opinion sans être agressé par celle qu'on tente de lui imposer.

Une importante innovation sociale dans la presse mauricienne serait d'introduire dans les contenus journalistiques une distinction claire entre ce qui relève du factuel, ce qui relève de l'opinion et ce qui relève de l'analyse. Trop souvent, on constate un amalgame entre opinion et analyse, des articles d'opinion se présentant comme des analyses, tandis que les analyses dignes de ce nom font encore cruellement défaut. Cette distinction entre faits, opinions et analyses

---

[29] Ibid.
[30] Michael Schudson, *op. cit.,* p. 38.
[31] Catherine Boudet, « Chronique. Plus responsables », *Impact* n°1 du 12 mars 2010.

est fondamentale pour permettre une véritable construction des savoirs collectifs permettant de fonder une citoyenneté mauricienne éclairée, car seule cette distinction permet au lecteur d'être en mesure de construire sa propre échelle de valeurs et sa grille de lecture de l'actualité, et donc à terme, de dialoguer constructivement.

5

L'Intégrité des Institutions Publiques: Le cas de la MBC

Dan Callikan
Directeur Général de la MBC[32]

Le texte qui suit est une transcription faite à partir d'un enregistrement audio de l'intervenant.

Pour que les institutions fonctionnent correctement, il faut tout d'abord une bonne gestion ('management'), c'est la base même de la bonne gouvernance. Il est clair que l'île Maurice s'intègre dans un monde global et sera jugée de plus en plus par rapport à ces critères.

L'intégrité des institutions est donc fondamentale. Pour cela, deux conditions essentielles doivent être remplies :

1. Il faut que la loi soit appliquée
2. Il faut y avoir le respect de la loi et des procédures

Il faut que chacun sache quelle est sa responsabilité et quelle est l'étendue de son pouvoir et dans quels paramètres il peut agir. Cela concerne aussi bien les individus que les institutions.

Il faut que ceux qui dirigent les institutions aient la volonté de faire respecter l'institution. C'est un principe de base. L'éthique personnelle est aussi importante.

Pour que les institutions fonctionnent, pour que la loi fonctionne correctement, il faut que les personnes qui sont en position de faire appliquer la loi ou de faire fonctionner la loi et les procédures aient la volonté de le faire dans la clarté et dans la transparence.

---

[32] Mauritius Broadcasting Corporation

Le travail actuel au niveau de la MBC

Pour qu'une institution ait la capacité de faire respecter la loi qui la gouverne (par exemple, la MBC) il faut qu'elle ait une administration digne de ce nom. Il faut que la structure administrative existe et il faut qu'il y ait des pratiques administratives claires au sein de l'entreprise.

Il fallait donc mener une action pour remettre sur pied une administration, pour que les chefs de service et le personnel sachent exactement quelles sont leurs responsabilités, leurs devoirs et dans quels paramètres ils travaillent. Si à l'intérieur même de l'institution cela n'existe pas, c'est peine perdue de penser que l'institution se fera respecter et pourra accomplir sa mission dans de bonnes conditions car sa mission est une mission de service public tout en faisant en sorte qu'il y ait le meilleur produit possible qui soit mis à la disposition du public d'une part sur le plan des informations (crédibles) et d'autre part sur le plan d'une production locale variée et de qualité.

Pour que la discipline prévale, il faut que chacun sache quoi faire dans cette entreprise, qu'il y ait une relation acceptable entretenue entre les personnes. (Par exemple, fumer ou consommer des boissons alcoolisées ne peut être toléré sur le lieu de travail). Il faut avoir le respect de son lieu de travail et de son outil de travail. C'est le minimum que l'on peut attendre de quelqu'un qui travaille dans une institution. C'est le genre de choses qui a dû être imposé car la discipline au travail n'existait plus au sein de l'institution. Tout cela est dû à une administration qui était tombée en panne elle-même.

Il faut savoir que 52% des ressources à la MBC vont aux salaires et allocations des personnels, ce qui est extrêmement élevé pour n'importe quelle organisation. Les revenus étaient en baisse constante (e.g. le marketing).

Tout est lié. Si la qualité des films, des séries ou des programmes laisse à désirer, s'il n'y a pas un choix qui est fait avec une vision claire sur le genre de films, séries ou programmes que l'on veut avoir, le genre de produit qu'on veut donner à la population, forcément le taux d'audience va baisser avec des conséquences sur la publicité. Il fallait donc inverser la tendance.

La publicité

Même si la MBC est en situation de monopole, il faut se rendre compte que les entreprises ont le choix quand à leur support publicitaire. Dorénavant, nous avons les radios, les *billboards*, les journaux et autres. La MBC n'est plus une nécessité. Il faut devenir pro-actif et aller vers les entreprises en leur faisant prendre conscience de la programmation améliorée. C'est ce qu'on fait depuis une année et je crois que là, les résultats sont positifs.

Sur le plan de l'information il faut dire que ce secteur a connu une transformation. Avant, je pense que le public le reconnaîtra, l'information était institutionnelle, c'est-à-dire, qu'on allait couvrir les événements organisés par des ministères, etc. On passait son temps cloîtré à Port-Louis.

Sur 40 minutes d'information, 25 minutes étaient consacrées à des déclarations ministérielles. Une situation pareille est inacceptable et ce n'est pas étonnant que la crédibilité de la station était au plus bas. C'est ce qui nous a amené à transformer l'information et nous avons fait en sorte que l'information institutionnelle ne représente qu'une partie du bulletin d'information et que ce bulletin soit ouvert aux Mauriciens, pour montrer ce qui se passe dans les régions, aller voir les petits entrepreneurs pour faire leurs interviews, montrer ce qu'ils sont en train de réaliser et donc s'ouvrir sur la population mauricienne et montrer ce pays en marche dans différents domaines. C'est une transformation radicale. Cela ne peut pas se faire du jour au lendemain. Il faut avoir la volonté d'assurer une information ouverte pour que le public soit satisfait car la MBC est une institution nationale qui doit fonctionner pour tout le public qui paye la redevance.

La crédibilité

Pour obtenir le respect de l'institution il faut déjà retrouver la crédibilité, il faut que le public sente qu'il y a une direction qui est en train de faire bouger les choses afin de satisfaire ses aspirations : à plus d'ouverture sans aucun doute et à un *entertainment* qui soit diversifié et qui puisse lui donner satisfaction. C'est à partir de là que peut être établie une relation plus étroite avec le public, dans le sens d'une meilleure programmation et d'une meilleure qualité des programmes. Il y a là un gros travail à faire.

Une autre valeur que la direction veut apporter au personnel de la MBC, c'est de le responsabiliser par rapport à son propre travail, c'est-à-dire que chacun doit faire son travail au mieux de ses possibilités. Je dois dire, par exemple, qu'il n'y a plus depuis longtemps de technicien pour la lumière ni de technicien pour le son à la MBC. Vous êtes confronté à la réalité: comment améliorer la qualité des programmes locaux sans ces compétences? Depuis quelque temps, il y a eu une forte diminution des programmes locaux. Ces programmes avaient été remplacés par des produits importés. Aujourd'hui il faut refaire tout cela, mettre les moyens pour refaire de bonnes productions.

Le respect de l'institution face aux forces extérieures n'est que le prolongement du respect des normes inculquées à l'intérieur de l'institution. Cela demande une volonté, une vision pour l'appliquer. Ce n'est pas facile de transformer quand les mauvaises habitudes ont été prises. Faire évoluer le comportement du personnel prend plus de temps et demande plus de patience.

Pour nous faire respecter au niveau de la campagne électorale, nous avons eu des conflits avec l'opposition officielle dont nous avons d'ailleurs un représentant ici. Ils sont allés à l'Independant Broadcasting Authority (IBA) pour protester énergiquement contre ce qu'ils appelaient le saucissonnage de leur programme. J'ai donné tous les enregistrements sur DVD à l'IBA qui les a étudiés et a conclu qu'il n'y avait aucun saucissonnage. L'IBA a donc rejeté les plaintes de l'opposition officielle. Cette dernière a aussi protesté auprès des observateurs de la SADC (Southern African Development Community). La SADC avait également déclaré que la MBC avait respecté les règlements et donné un *'level-playing field'* à tout le monde.

En ce qu'il s'agit du conflit actuel avec le ministre du travail qui a convoqué directement le directeur des ressources humaines de la MBC sans passer par le directeur général, ceci est inacceptable. Le directeur des ressources humaines n'est donc pas allé à sa réunion. Le lendemain, le ministre m'a appelé et m'a affirmé qu'il voulait 'clear the air'. Je lui ai rappelé la nécessité de suivre les règlements et la procédure.

Nous avons d'ailleurs considéré que les bases légales sur lesquelles le ministre s'est appuyé pour servir la convocation ne sont pas valides.

L'affaire est maintenant devant la cour industrielle et la commission de conciliation. C'est bon que les institutions continuent à jouer leur rôle et que les institutions judiciaires et de contrôle soient appelées et qu'elles puissent donner leur point de vue sur ce conflit légal.

Car le respect de la loi et des règlements constitue la base de la démocratie et de la bonne gouvernance.

Il faut que tous ceux qui sont chargés de l'application des lois et règlements aient le courage et la volonté nécessaires pour les faire respecter.

6

Radios Privées: Entre impératifs commerciaux et service public

Abdoullah Earally
Journaliste à Radio Plus[33]

Le texte qui suit est une transcription faite à partir d'un enregistrement audio de l'intervenant.

La question du jour concerne l'équilibre qu'il doit y avoir entre les impératifs commerciaux et un service pour le public, qu'apportent les radios privées.

J'ai décliné ma présentation en quatre thèmes:

• Équilibre dans le paysage médiatique nouveau où chacun doit trouver sa part de marché.

• Équilibre sur l'information à donner aux auditeurs. Il s'agit là d'éviter l'overdose de certains types d'informations, de respecter la pluralité et les voix des différents horizons, et de faire attention pour bien équilibrer en matière de couverture politique.

• Équilibre sur la participation des auditeurs. Il faut ici éviter le piège de l'instrumentalisation des radios par les auditeurs et autres acteurs de la société, et éviter l'excès d'interaction.

• Équilibre entre les impératifs commerciaux et la radio, c'est-à-dire, la publicité et le journalisme. Il n'y pas là nécessairement de

---

[33] Abdoollah Earally est désormais journaliste à La Sentinelle

contradiction. Il suffit de savoir comment opérer.

(1) Équilibre dans le paysage médiatique

D'emblée, je voudrais parler de la Mauritius Broadcasting Corporation (MBC). Malheureusement, la radio-télévision nationale n'a pas assez évolué et reste anachronique et très loin des évolutions du monde. Les chaînes de la télévision publique sont encore inféodées au pouvoir.

En même temps, il s'agit d'une mission immense pour une radio-télévision publique, soit faire de la pédagogie pour expliquer ce qui se passe dans la pays et ne pas tout peindre en noir. La mission de la MBC comprend une large palette d'activités: promouvoir l'éducation, la promotion de la qualité, la fiabilité de l'information et non la désinformation. En plus, il faut des programmes culturels, religieux, musicaux qui respectent la pluralité des langues et cultures et, comme on le sait, c'est très compliqué dans un pays comme Maurice.

Mais, la MBC reçoit des fonds; ils ont la redevance, ils ont de la publicité contrairement à des pays où la publicité est mieux règlementée sur les médias nationaux mais la MBC a cette possibilité et c'est une très belle chance.

Quant à la radio commerciale, elle a tout de suite marqué la différence par un ton et un contenu nouveau, une nouvelle manière de faire du journalisme au sens le plus large parce qu'on ne fait pas ce métier aujourd'hui comme on le faisait dix ou vingt ans de cela. Des programmes, de l'animation ou des news qui collent plus à la réalité de la rue et du pays car il faut donner la possibilité à la rue de s'exprimer et aussi lui donner plus d'ouverture.

Les radios privées sont venues apporter cette complémentarité qui manquait non seulement dans l'audiovisuel mais dans l'ensemble du paysage médiatique.

Quelqu'un a dit une fois que c'est 'la parole libérée'. C'est vrai car la radio est plus spontanée, naturelle, directe et plus facile aussi pour les auditeurs. Auparavant avec la presse écrite, pour que l'auditeur puisse s'exprimer, il fallait d'abord qu'il ait une petite maîtrise de la langue française, ce qui était intimidant pour lui, mais aujourd'hui avec la radio il peut s'exprimer et les Mauriciens s'expriment bien et savent ce qu'ils doivent dire en public. Il y a eu parfois des moments délicats mais 99% des auditeurs savent quel discours ils doivent tenir en public.

Les radios privées sont donc venues répondre à cette attente, ce qui amène un équilibre dans la participation du public dans la vie des médias avec l'avènement des radios privées.

En plus il y a le divertissement qui est nouveau aujourd'hui, il y a la différence qui se joue sur l'information qui est plus dynamique. Vous sentez ce dynamisme car l'information est actualisée d'heure en heure et c'est plus facile pour les radios que la télévision du à la logistique. Cela marche fort car le public s'est tout de suite accroché à ces nouveaux médias. Ces radios font aussi de l'événementiel, du sensationnel parfois, je l'admets, et aussi du spectacle.

Ce qu'elles ne font pas pour l'instant (en espérant que cela va venir), c'est '*l'infotainment*' pour éviter l'effritement car il y a cette répétition qu'on entend en ce moment sur les radios, qui devient un peu lourd. Mais cela devrait venir.

(2) L'overdose de faits divers
Aussi, on raconte ce qui se passe dans le pays mais on s'est rendu compte que si on ne fait pas attention, l'auditeur sera blasé.

Les radios privées sont là pour:

• Exprimer la pluralité dans les informations. C'est ce qu'on fait tous les jours.

• Éviter d'entrer dans le jeu des hommes politiques. Mais je l'admets aussi: on fait aussi de temps en temps de la politique politicienne car les médias institutionnels auront du mal à le faire et c'est un créneau qui est bien exploité par les médias du privé.

L'équilibre est vital à ce niveau. Les radios d'État font de l'institutionnel (par exemple, inaugurations par des ministres). Les radios privées, elles, vont chercher l'info derrière l'info.

(3) Équilibre sur la participation des auditeurs

Il faut éviter l'instrumentalisation car l'auditeur n'est pas bête. Il est intelligent, malin et par moments, il nous manipule aussi et on fait attention à cela. Il nous est tout de même arrivé par moments de tomber sur des auditeurs qui ne sont pas sérieux et qui savent utiliser la radio pour faire passer leur message à eux dans des secteurs très particuliers.

On essaie de faire très attention contrairement à ce qui se passe dans certaines radios ailleurs (Radio Freedom à l'île de la Réunion par exemple). Ce genre de radio ne serait pas apprécié à Maurice car sur ces radios, les auditeurs appellent et disent ce qu'ils veulent même si quelquefois les infos ne sont pas exactes. A la Réunion, Radio Freedom est devenue une référence et un phénomène de société. Quelques services publics comme la police ou les pompiers apprennent qu'il y a un accident à travers Freedom car ils sont plus branchés sur Freedom que sur les autres médias ou sur leur propre réseau.

Parfois ce genre de choses arrive à Maurice où les policiers appellent pour s'informer des problèmes dont ils ont entendu parler à travers les auditeurs. Mais ici nous avons des filets de protection car nous prenons l'information, les coordonnées et la source de l'information. On vérifie l'information et c'est uniquement après que l'on va diffuser, contrairement à Freedom. Le contrôle est vital car la crédibilité va dépendre de ce que vous allez donner comme information.

(4) Les impératifs commerciaux

Tous les journalistes qui ont une certaine expérience savent qu'il faut respecter un code de déontologie même si ce n'est pas écrit par les instances de régulation comme l'Independant Broadcasting Authority (IBA), du moins dans les détails, mais il est écrit dans les grandes lignes. Mais pour les journalistes, nous savons que ce code est appliqué généralement mais il y a des intérêts financiers car la radio doit faire des profits. Pour Radio Plus, la qualité de son service justifie son succès. Si elle est populaire, c'est en raison de la qualité de son service.

Pour moi les radios privées, c'est encore une aventure nouvelle. Nous avons toujours besoin d'atteindre notre vitesse de croisière pour plus de stabilité.

Je terminerai sur une citation de Marie-Soleil Frère, chargée de cours à l'Université Libre de Bruxelles: « Mieux vaut habituer les populations d'Afrique centrale à des mots libres, diversifiés et contradictoires, même s'ils sont parfois maladroits, excessifs ou vendus, plutôt qu'à des mots d'ordre tous uniformes, voire tous en uniforme. »

7

21st Century Broadcasting: The Need to Reinvent and Revisit Established Systems. The Case of Mauritius

Roukaya Kasenally
University of Mauritius

The end of the 20th Century saw an exponential growth in the presence and use of the media and as we end the first decade of the 21st Century, most of us are overwhelmed by the sheer power of new media to reshape and redefine the political, cultural and social contours of our society. In fact, what was known as the liberalization of airwaves only really took off in the early 1990s (see Noam 1991 and Thussu 2006) - meaning that in relatively two short decades our media system has transformed itself from being a novelty to an everyday feature of our life.

There are a number of features that made this possible such as market liberalization and the loosening of government control and monopoly, diversity in content production and distribution. However, the one feature that is believed to have changed the face of media is technology. Indeed, technology is responsible for making media affordable (to the many more instead of the little few), available (from scarcity (analogue) to unlimited (digital)), convergent (one platform with multiple uses) and of course instantaneous and in real time.

Contemporary literature on media systems do not tend to discriminate between the various types of media as we are inevitably living in an era of convergence where the press, radio, television, the internet and telecommunications are aiming at the same audience by offering competing products. However, for the purpose of this paper the emphasis will essentially be on the traditional broadcasting systems where the line of demarcation has been between a public service model as opposed to a commercial one. The debate is shifting and there is a need to develop a sort of 'hybrid' model that retains the core values of public service and the appeal of commercial broadcasting. This paper makes particular reference to the case of Mauritius where till today there remains a clear separation between public and private media leading quite often to a highly polarized setup in the manner in which media content is produced, transmitted and ultimately consumed on the island.

Key Concepts in Broadcasting

As mentioned above the old and established paradigm in which broadcasting operated was the ideological divide between public service and that of the commercial. In fact, the divide was not merely ideological but also geographical – Western Europe as opposed to the United States.

When television emerged in the early 1950s in Western Europe it had a very strong statist approach where broadcasting was centralized in a public institution with a monopoly over radio and television. Overtime the statist model was loosened and gave way to the public service notion where broadcasting was essentially seen as a public good that had to adhere to a set of core values to inform, educate and entertain the nation especially after World War 2. Different countries across Western Europe experienced with different aspects of the public service model such as mixed financing (license fee and advertising revenues), duopolistic tradition and the investment into creating quality programs that were culturally and politically influential.

Across the Atlantic, the experience was quite different as the main aim was to develop broadcasting into a lucrative business and from the very onset this was the main trait that defined American broadcasting as is aptly captured in the following statement:

"The revenue and income growth of the commercial broadcasting industry has far outstripped the average for all industries in the past and should continue to do so during the next five years and even beyond."

(Clift and Greer 1981: 51)

Despite these being still very early days of the commercial experience in the United States, it clearly demonstrated the main motivation and till today, the United States' broadcasting system remains highly commercial. Today's broadcasting market has significantly altered the differences between the public service and commercial model and this has been essentially triggered by the advent of technology. Technology has in fact allowed for the displacement of traditional media networks as they have created the potential for a large number of broadcasting channels. For instance, in the US where cable technologies started operating earlier than in most European countries, there are now several new general broadcasters with schedules that cover a range of program types and which have now achieved the threshold audience numbers to appear in the A.C Nielsen year- end summaries: FOX, United Paramount Network and Warner Bros (Hargreaves-Heap, 2005). Similar patterns can be noted in Europe, India and Australia among other countries. There have been different strategies/responses by the established networks ranging from 'copycatting' successful satellite/cable networks, affirming ferociously their broadcast exceptionalism (BBC) to developing and experiencing with hybrid systems. In the process there have been a number of impacts namely on: the financing of broadcasting, the types of programs commissioned and broadcast and on the audience.

Financing and Funding Broadcasting

Not only is there much more to read, listen, watch and play with but increasingly such content is becoming freely available to larger sections of the audience. This as expected has had effects on the older and more established systems that not only had a 'guaranteed' audience share but also a regular source of money either through the license fee or advertising revenues. In fact, this regular and practically 'uninterrupted' source of funding allowed many of the established systems to pursue a particular tradition of broadcasting (public service or commercial) and also to develop some highly monopolistic and protectionist approaches when it came to the production and diffusion of certain type of broadcasting materials. Gone are such days as what is increasingly being defined as the broadcast marketplace with a crowded group of players.

The license fee is a form of tax used by many countries to support indigenous broadcasting industries. The fee is levied on the television receiver set and paid at regular intervals. The BBC is the institution that till date embodies best the spirit behind the license fee as it has allowed the institution to preserve its public service mandate as envisioned by Lord Reith at its inception days:

> "The license fee system involves each member of the viewing public...in the feeling that he is entitled to a direct say in what he gets for his money. At the same time, the license fee system puts the broadcasters in a more direct relationship with the public than any other system of financing would. It reinforces a frame of mind in the BBC which impels us constantly to ask ourselves the question: 'What ought we to be doing to serve the public better?'"
>
> (Curran 2002: 22)

The value of such a system for supporting a nation's broadcasting has three aspects. First, it assigns the costs for broadcasting directly to its consumers. Second, this tends to create a mutual and reciprocal sense of responsibility between the broadcasters and the audience members which, third, frees the broadcasters from control and influence by governments (as might be the case where direct government support exists) or advertisers (as might be the case in commercial systems). Against these benefits is the problem of complacency. An increasing number of nations with license fees also allow limited commercial broadcasting, in part to overcome this tendency. Many countries other than Great Britain, including Israel,

54

Malta, France, the Netherlands and Jordan, have some form of license fees. Two thirds of the countries in Europe, one half in Africa and Asia and 10% of those in the Americas and Caribbean rely, at least in part, on a license fee to support their television systems. Common among them is a philosophy of broadcasting that sees it as a "public good."

Despite it promoting and sustaining a particular 'brand' of broadcasting, the obligatory license fee is increasingly becoming difficult to justify especially when there is large amount of free content available. The debate has been particularly intense in the United Kingdom where the flagship of British broadcasting - the BBC is coming under attack for its privileged access and use of the license fee. The 2010 MacTaggart lecture (a yearly keynote of the Edinburgh International Television Festival) was delivered by the Managing Director of the BBC Mark Thompson and the latter made a forceful case for the continued relevance of the BBC by proposing a series of fundamental changes to the core structure of the BBC. Whether these core changes will satisfy the detractors of the BBC is yet to be witnessed but one thing that is clear is that the manner in which broadcasting matters are conducted will never be the same – gone are the days of acquired right or unchallenged champion!

Types of Programmes Commissioned/Broadcast

Earlier the point was made about the fact that the broadcast environment was becoming increasingly crowded. Indeed there is so much more to see but at the same time we are witnessing a culture of sameness and a growing sense of program conformity. Despite calls for greater diversity and plurality, these calls are very often voiced through the prism of sheer multitude – as long as you have more on offer this is supposed to de facto bring about greater choice. Another notable feature is the sense of populism that is driving the public service agenda. In fact, established broadcasting institutions like the BBC are going popular and populist to appeal to the public. In fact, this 'move' towards greater populist fare is due to the widespread belief that public service broadcasting is generally condescending, high brow and out of touch with the public's wants and demands whilst commercial broadcasting is more entertaining and has a common touch appeal. There is no doubt that this necessary shift in program format and content has been the cause of numerous tensions in what one can call national/generalist broadcasting systems. There was the need to go popular but not compromise on the essential core principles of public service broadcasting: objectivity, credibility, balance and truthfulness. This was particularly important when it came to production, representation and diffusion of news and other factual content:

> *"It must furnish news that is objective and impartial, it must provide for discussion and debate that fairly reflects a wide range of views. It must be creative and energetic in ensuring that every citizen gets a chance to join in. And in all these areas we need to know that the programme makers are attempting to find and tell us the truth of the matter. They may not always succeed. They must always try."*
>
> (Attenborough, 2009)

Unlike national/generalist broadcast providers, private/specialist ones have greater leeway and flexibility when it comes to content. Over the last decade and a half, we have witnessed a real explosion in the number of specialist/thematic channels ranging from 24 hour shopping to history channels. These are premium channels that are accessible through subscription or Pay TV and very often are of interest to fewer as opposed to more viewers.

The Audience: The Rise of Public Commissioning

There have been two fundamental changes to the concept of the audience. Firstly, the audience is far from being this passive and inert body but on the contrary has defined its demands and expectations in an increasingly articulate and interactive manner. Secondly, the audience is now a plural concept reflecting both diversity and fragmentation in their demands/expectations. The audience has always been an important feature of the broadcast equation as the latter is instrumental to the viability and sustainability of the broadcast industry – be it through the license fee or commercial model. In fact, in the commercial model the role/status of the audience is at times exaggerated when certain types of programmes are commissioned/aired to fit advertisement and or sponsorship audience profiles. This type of advertisement/sponsorship driven programs has often been the cause of the rather generalist understanding: that the viewers are being served what they want/like and this has been particularly visible along sensationalist media fare.

When relating to the idea of the audience within the broadcast environment, one is inevitably reminded of the term public. The term public and by extension 'publicness' denotes the role and responsibility that individual citizens/viewers and more specifically when it comes to the use of public money (public service model). Hind (2011) makes a forceful case of the 'return of the public' to develop a 'public system of knowledge through the process of public commissioning':

"Here citizens would collectively and equally make decisions about the allocation of resources to journalists and researchers. This allows for a platform/space where common deliberation allowing the public to address conditions of steepening inequality and deepening social distress" (pg 121)

Hind pursues his justification for 'public commissioning' by stressing on the point that 'over time the communication resources of the state would be brought under democratic control and a system currently used to shape popular perceptions and insulate elite decision making would give citizens some share in the creation of their own beliefs' (pg 141).

There is no doubt that Hind's argument and justification for a greater involvement/participation of the public is a major shift from the conventional idea of the distanced and disengaged audience member, blissfully consuming what was fed to it in terms of information, education and entertainment by broadcasters.

Mauritius: The Changing Media Landscape

Mauritian broadcasting has been shaped and influenced by its colonial experience. The main broadcasting station the Mauritius Broadcasting Corporation (MBC) was set up on the 8th June 1964 when the island was still a British colony. Like many then British colonies, Mauritian broadcasting was infused with the public service model and adopted the license fee as its main funding/financing model. The main motivation behind the setting up of the MBC as the public broadcaster was to build a sense of nationhood and prepare the islanders to embrace independence (that happened in 1968). Nearly half a century since its creation the MBC remains the sole provider of television services on the island. In fact, in 2002, broadcasting was partially liberalized and allowed for the setting up of three private commercial radio stations. It is interesting to note that unlike the broadcast media, print media in Mauritius is extremely diverse and varied and to a great extent unregulated. This offers at times a rather skewed media landscape with free, open and unregulated written media as opposed to a closed and highly regulated broadcast media.

The MBC: Public or State Broadcaster?

As stipulated by the MBC Act (1982), the MBC is defined as a public service broadcaster, whose main aim is 'to educate, entertain and inform the public'. In addition to that, the MBC Act 1982 emphasizes on a mandate of 'impartiality' and 'balance' when it comes to the production and representation of news and information. Unfortunately, the impartiality (especially political) track record of the MBC has been quite tainted and is the source of concern among a number of stakeholders. This brings one to actually question the status of the MBC – is it actually a state broadcaster cloaked in the public service garb? In fact, the case of the MBC would not be different from a number of 'public' broadcasters across the African continent that have been 'hijacked' by those in power to become their official mouthpiece. However, what is reassuring is that the winds of liberalization are blowing across the African continent forcing many of the old and ailing state broadcasters to reposition themselves in the broadcast marketplace or run the risk of losing their audience.

As mentioned earlier, the MBC exerts a monopolistic presence and control of the visual broadcast landscape and has been doing so for the last five decades. There is no doubt that the MBC has evolved considerably both at the technical and content level – successfully managed its digital switchover and in the process providing a host of new thematic channels (Knowledge Channel, Movie Channel, Tourism and Culture Channel). Only recently (October 2010), the MBC inaugurated its dedicated 'language channels' (Mandarin, Marathi, Tamil, Telegu and Urdu) in line with the MBC policy to produce and broadcast progammes in the languages spoken and understood by the Mauritian population.

Research has pointed to the fact that a fair majority of the audience turn to television as their primary source of information/news. Indeed, news constitutes an important feature of the viewers/listeners/readers media diet and most of them expect to access as much as possible unbiased, objective and balanced news/information. This is especially relevant in a media environment where alternative media and choices are becoming available and accessible to many more people as opposed to fewer people.

Unfortunately, the MBC has over the decades developed an entrenched culture of political bias and partiality to those who are in power and this is most visible when it comes to the presentation and representation of news. Certain observers attribute this overt sense of loyalty often bordering on subservience on the fact that it is the Prime Minister that appoints the director, chairperson and members of the MBC board. Although this can partly explain the prevailing culture of political bias and partiality, there seems to be a tacit understanding among those working at the MBC (from the management level to the body of journalists) that they must in no way displease those in power.

As expected, this state of affairs at the MBC, where some 60 percent of its finance/funding comes from the license fee has been a source of tension and at time outrage among the general public, the Opposition party and other civil society organizations. The chorus of discontent becomes more vocal during elections when the MBC is unashamedly used/abused by the incumbents. Over the years there has been a number of debates/discussions about ensuring that the MBC performs its role as a public provider of news/information in the most unbiased and objective manner. Unfortunately, these debates have been essentially concentrated around the election period (where political bias and partiality is at its peak) and once those who have been in Opposition access the realms of power they also abuse the system. Such a situation points to a certain lack of political commitment to transform a system that inherently serves those in power and not those that pay the license fee – the public.

Private Television: The Solution?

As mentioned in an earlier section, the Mauritian broadcast landscape is only partially liberalized with the coming in operation in 2002 of three private commercial radio stations. There is no doubt that these three private radio stations have considerably altered the broadcast setup in terms of choice, program formats and more interestingly brought about a real explosion in vox populi. Indeed, prior to that public radio or television operated along a top down approach with very little interaction from the public. Private radios from their onset privileged a form of communication/exchange with the listeners that ensured a participatory approach and many phone-in programs were devised in mind to get them to voice out on a range of issues. Over time, these private radio stations have become platforms for popular voicing out and in the process have started to instill a culture of debate. The area that has particularly benefited is that of political discussion and commentary where a diversity of views and opinions have been welcomed. As one would expect this state of affairs is in stark comparison to the type of political debate/commentary available on the MBC.

Therefore the question that warrants an answer – has the presence of these private radio stations caused the MBC to amend its monopolistic policy? Well the answer is rather nuanced as the MBC (radio and television) has responded to competition from these private radios by increasing the number of channels (greatly aided by the advent of digital technology) and diversifying content especially in the case of local production (currently accounts for 30 percent of overall content). However, the area which has witnessed no change (on the contrary has worsened) is that of political bias and partiality in the reporting and presentation of news and information.

Is the advent of private television then the answer to a more competitive and balanced visual broadcast media? In fact, subscription TV and other cable channels have been available to viewers who can afford them since more than a decade and a half and its penetration within the Mauritian household has been quite spectacular as for a population of 1.3 million, there are 90 000 Pay TV subscribers (Telecoms, Internet and Broadcasting in Africa, 2010). For a number of years now, the need for local private television network has been at the centre of discussion. The Independent Broadcasting Authority (IBA) Act (2000) (responsible for the licensing and regulation of broadcast services in Mauritius) makes provision for the licences to private television operators, although it limits foreign shareholding to 20 percent only. On a number of occasions, the current Prime Minister Navin Ramgoolam has indicated his government's inclination to totally liberalize the broadcast airwaves by allowing for the provision of private television – the latter even appears in the electoral manifesto of the ruling coalition. However, where the real test lies is in the capacity of transforming the rhetoric of good intention into that of action. Also the required thought will have to be given as to the most appropriate funding/financial model as well as ensure that impartiality and balance in news reporting and production remain cornerstone features.

The Way Forward

The 21st century is no doubt one of great social, cultural and technological mutations. Media consumers are quickly migrating to new and alternative platforms. Old, established and hierarchical systems are either becoming extinct or having to fundamentally rethink and reinvent themselves. The case of Mauritius is interesting as it clearly positions itself as an innovative provider of information and knowledge as well as a democratic exemplar within the African subcontinent. If the island wishes to stay true to this image, it is imperative that it breaks the last barrier and complete the full process of liberalization. As for the MBC, once the market forces of broadcast liberalization have been unleashed it will have no other means to realign itself to the demands and expectations of the audience.

References

Attenborough R (2009) 'The Future of Public Service Broadcasting' (http://www.scribd.com/doc/22601976/The-Future- of-Public-Service-Broadcasting)

Clift C and Greer A (1981) Broadcast Programming; The Current Perspectives. University Press of America

Curran J (2002) Media and Power. Routledge

Hargreaves-Heap S P (2005) Television in a Digital Age: What Role for public Service Broadcasting', Economic Policy, Volume 20: Issue 41

Hind D (2011) the Return of the Public. Verso Publication

Independent Broadcasting Authority (2000). Laws of Mauritius: Government of Mauritius

Mauritius Broadcasting Authority (1982). Laws of Mauritius: Government of Mauritius

Noam E (1991) Television in Europe. Oxford University Press

Thussu D (2006) International Communication: Continuity and Change. Hodder Arnold

8

The Role of Regulation

Gilbert Ithier
Chairman of the Complaints Committee of the IBA

The following text was transcribed from an audio recording of the speaker's presentation.

The purpose of the courts and tribunals is to avoid chaos. One can imagine the disruptive effect if people were to be allowed to settle disputes amongst themselves. Hence the need for the State to provide mechanisms to allow people to argue their cases and have their disputes adjudicated upon in a fair and respectful manner. To do this, the courts need to refer to a piece of legislation.

For our field, it is the Independent Broadcasting Authority Act which was enacted in 2000 and came into force by promulgation as from the 1st January 2001.

The purpose of this Act is twofold:

1. It provides for the creation of a complaints committee, the tribunal, which will hear and determine matters or grievances by members of public against radio broadcasters.

2. It gives power to the authority to regulate the service providers.

The committee is in fact a tribunal, an informal one, so that members of the public may feel at ease. Its main purpose is to make it easier for laymen to come before the chair to explain their case, where simple procedures are made available.

Who can actually come before the IBA? Any person/member of the public who feels aggrieved by a comment, criticism or programme on any radio can lodge a complaint, by filing a simple letter to the Complaints Committee at the IBA premises or a standard complaint form on the IBA website. We then call the radio to respond to the grievances. We organise a hearing with both parties. The parties may or may not be represented by a lawyer at the hearing to be made. This is an advantage compared to a court of law. In a tribunal, you can come alone and you will be helped by the chair to explain your case.

The other question is whether anybody can file a complaint. The requirement is that the person must be directly affected by the comment, but this requirement is quite difficult to interpret. For example, a few months ago we had a case of Mr X making a speech at a political party before elections and being severely criticised for his speech by the radio broadcaster. The complaint came, not from Mr X, but from the party on whose behalf he was speaking. I must add that he eventually did not turn out to be a candidate for the party. I drew attention to the counsel that the person aggrieved had not made any complaint. He then withdrew the case.

The person aggrieved should be the only one making the complaint and not somebody else on his behalf. The time limit is 6 months as from the date on which the programme was broadcast.

On what basis can a person make a complaint? There are three possible grounds:

- There is unfair treatment of the person in the program.

- There is an infringement or likelihood of infringement of privacy by radio broadcasters while collecting information for a program.

- There is a breach of the code of ethics (this code is being finalised and will soon be in force).[34].

To date, all cases we have had so far are based on the first two grounds of course.

An important provision of the law is that if the complaint is going to be heard by or is likely to be a subject matter before a court of law, then the IBA is precluded from hearing the case. We have had two such instances, one currently before us. We have to decide whether we can proceed based on whether it is going to be entirely separate or if there is intermingling. In the second case, we do not hear the matter.

We also do not entertain complaints of a frivolous or vexatious nature.

It should be pointed out that Complaints Committee and the Authority are two separate bodies. The Complaints Committee is a tribunal. It takes decisions, hears cases, and gives hearing and rulings independently of the Authority. But we cannot publish our decisions directly; these need to be forwarded to the Authority which will eventually communicate these to the concerned parties.

As for the Authority, it exercises a regulatory function. Section 5 of the IBA Act states that the Authority can monitor radio programs, can establish guidelines and can take sanctions against radio providers which do not abide by the terms and conditions laid down in their licence. The licences are granted by the Authority which actually sets out the terms and conditions.

If one of the service providers does not abide by the terms and conditions, the Authority can take sanctions of varied nature. Usually they are directed to be careful in the future and make sure that this state of affair does not recur. The ultimate sanction being the removal of the license altogether (which has fortunately not happened so far).

---

[34] The Code of Ethics has since been finalised and is available on the IBA's website at www.iba.mu

Finally, the second schedule of the Act refers to the code of conduct which applies to the radio broadcasters, whereby the authority sets out the general rules with regard to the observance of not publishing or airing obscene matters, matters which may affect the sensibility of people on their religious beliefs.

So, the Act provides the framework for the operation of radio broadcasters. I personally believe that the Act is a fair one.

9

L'Auto-Régulation: Le Code de Conduite de la NEPA

Lindsay Rivière
Directeur de Business Publications & Président de la NEPA

Le texte qui suit est une transcription faite à partir d'un enregistrement audio de l'intervenant.

Faut-il réglementer davantage la presse? Qui doit le faire? La presse doit- elle s'auto-réglementer? Quelle doit être l'étendue de la législation et de cette intervention?

Il existe une perception à Maurice que la presse est un peu hors de contrôle et fonctionne dans un cadre législatif assez flou qui permet tous les excès, qu'il doit y avoir une réglementation plus sévère. Rien n'est plus faux. Il existe un cadre légal extrêmement sévère, extrêmement élaboré pour la presse mauricienne.

À l'occasion de la visite de Maître Geoffrey Robertson, conseiller du Premier Ministre sur les lois de la presse, nous avons pu lui présenter un condensé de toutes les lois affectant la presse à Maurice. Il s'agit d'un document de plus de 30 pages réglementant chaque activité de la presse à l'île Maurice avec des peines souvent très sévères. Bien sûr, ces lois ne sont souvent pas appliquées, d'où la perception d'un vacuum légal et que la presse est hors de contrôle. Mais il y a bien des réglementations concernant la sédition, la diffamation, de nombreux éléments du code pénal.

En sus de cela, depuis l'Indépendance, il y a eu de nombreuses tentatives dans la presse pour encadrer et réglementer le fonctionnement de la presse dans une démarche volontaire. En 1971, l'Association des Journalistes de L'île Maurice (AJIM) publiait déjà un code de conduite basé sur le modèle britannique et en collaboration avec des instances étrangères telles que la Commonwealth Press Union. Ce code a été circulé, adopté et couvrait toutes les normes professionnelles exigées et avait pour but de constituer une série de repères pour la déontologie. L'AJIM a duré une dizaine d'années, a regroupé toute la presse et a été présidée par des journalistes de calibre mais elle est, par la suite, morte de sa belle mort.

Ce code couvrait toutes les responsabilités des journalistes:

*   le respect de la vie privée,
*   le respect de la confidentialité des sources d'information,
*   le droit de réponse,
*   le souci de l'exactitude de l'information,
*   la dissociation de l'information et de l'opinion,
*   l'intimidation,
*   le harcèlement des individus,
*   l'intrusion dans le deuil et la douleur,
*   les droits de l'enfant et des malades, etc. Le code existe depuis plus de 30 ans déjà.

Il y a donc toujours eu une volonté d'encadrer la profession. Il y a aussi eu d'autres associations de presse ou de reporters (notamment celle présidée par Henri Marimootoo) avec un code similaire mais au succès inégal. Par la suite, il y eu la proposition d'un Press Council par le spécialiste britannique Kenneth Morgan (qu'a fait venir le Media Trust) mais qui n'a jamais été institué. Sa proposition était calquée sur le modèle britannique mais a été largement contestée car elle ne s'inspirait pas de la réalité mauricienne et ne prenait pas en compte les différentes sensibilités de la presse mauricienne. Pour l'essentiel, cette proposition passait par un Acte du parlement qui mettait en place une institution officielle. Une partie de la presse a cependant toujours été hostile à toute législation réglementant la profession.

Depuis, le Professeur Geoffrey Robertson a été invité pour essayer de codifier toutes les législations. Son rapport a été déposé et je crois comprendre qu'il reviendra bientôt. À la NEPA (Newspapers Editors and Publishers Association), nous l'avons rencontré et lui avons remis nos documents et propositions. Aucune ébauche de son rapport n'a cependant été reçue à ce jour.

La dernière tentative revient à la NEPA qui a été fondée il y a trois ans. Nous avons publié un code de conduite - vu, revu, adopté par l'ensemble de la profession. Il reprend les grands principes d'il y a 30 ans. La question est: est-ce que ce code sera appliqué? Est-ce qu'il est appliqué?

La presse mauricienne est favorable à l'auto-régulation mais elle est divisée sur l'introduction de nouvelles législations. Il y a d'ailleurs des difficultés associées à la question d'auto-régulation:

1. A l'intérieur de la presse qui n'est pas un bloc monolithique, il y a des opinions divergentes, ce qui gêne la mise en route de l'auto-régulation.

2. Il faut mettre en place un *Complaints Committee* de la NEPA. Un fort courant est pour la mise en place d'un comité interne à la NEPA, une sorte de tribunal de pairs avec des personnalités indépendantes ayant un bagage légal. La crainte est d'avoir un système de licences pour les journaux comme pour les radios si on laisse le parlement réglementer car qui octroie une licence peut la reprendre.

3. Il y a des problèmes de méfiance extrême entre la presse et les autorités qui ne jouent pas le jeu.

Or, il n'y a pas de mauvais journaux, il y a de mauvais rédacteurs en chef. Les journaux reflètent la qualité, les normes, les valeurs et principes et l'éthique de leurs responsables. Beaucoup de critiques devraient d'ailleurs être déposées aux pieds des conseils d'administration, des propriétaires et des directeurs et rédacteurs en chef. Malheureusement à Maurice, cette responsabilité n'est pas entièrement assumée. Les institutions ne valent que ce que valent les hommes qui les composent, comme l'a dit Dan Callikhan plus tôt. Ce n'est pas en mettant des lois qu'on règle des problèmes. Il faut responsabiliser les gens.

Il est dommage que le Media Trust, qui est censé former la profession, soit paralysé par des décisions gouvernementales alors que ce même gouvernement critique la qualité de la presse.

La question donc que l'on doit se poser: est-ce qu'il faut plus de lois ou plus de qualité?

Je le répète: la qualité de la presse passe par la qualité des hommes et des femmes qui la composent. Il faut aussi une introspection dans la profession. Avons-nous investi assez dans les hommes autant que dans les équipements? Faisons-nous assez en termes de formation? Les autorités font-elles ce qu'il faut en termes de dialogue.

La solution à nos problèmes n'est certainement pas d'introduire plus de lois!

10

State or Self Regulation: The Search for Common Ground

Christina Chan-Meetoo
Lecturer at the University of Mauritius

This paper attempts to chart the current status of relationships between the press and the State in Mauritius. Over the last five years, heated debates and conflicts have regularly erupted between these two sets of actors with little hope for level-headed resolution. Successive attempts from both sides at organising and strategising have all reaped little in terms of concrete measures to address the situation. This paper reviews the major events which have marked this long-lasting confrontation over the last decade, from the presentation of a proposal for a Press Council to that of a hypothetical Media Commission Bill. It examines the issue of regulation (or self-regulation) in the Mauritian press, the so-called Fourth Estate.

The context

The Mauritian mediascape is surprisingly vibrant and alive for a small island state of 1.2 million inhabitants. The written press in particular can boast of a rich and long history of participation in the local media sphere. The press has been in existence for more than two centuries, dating back to the colonial occupation of the island by the French. The first newspaper on the island, *Annonces, Affiches et Avis Divers*, a paper devoted to official announcements and advertisements, appeared in 1773 under the French colonial rule. But a free press was only promulgated in 1831 (Simonin, 2005) and *Le*

Cernéen was the first publication to have appeared as free press in 1832 and would thrive for 150 years.

Although the written press went through difficult times in the early 1970's when it had to face government censorship after the ethnic riots, today, the Republic of Mauritius can boast of a fairly free press with a very high number of publications on the market. In effect, Mauritius has one of the highest press density in the Francophone area with over seven hundred publications which have been in circulation since the beginning (Carter, 1998 cited in Lallmohamed, 2005) and currently, with some forty titles of various periodicity as listed by the Central Statistical Office.

Not all of these publications enjoy a high circulation and readership but the sheer variety still points to a written press that caters for generalist audiences as well as specialised audiences including ethnic, linguistic, social and political diversity of approaches.

In such a context, the local press is the focus of a lot of public attention and this is enhanced by the recurring bursts of heated debates in the public sphere about the role of the media in society and the perceived necessity to regulate the activities of journalists and editors. This runs counter to the generally accepted idea that the media form part of the public sphere as defined by Habermas and indeed play a central role within it as the media are considered as one of the primary engines of democracy.

There has been undeniable progress in Mauritius since the 1970's (when there was drastic government censorship) but also occasional regressions with overt threats to press freedom which have somewhat negatively impacted our international rankings (such as the Reporters Without Borders Index). On the one hand, the media space has been broadened with many new entrants on the market and an expanded audience. On the other, the tension between the State and the private media is cause for concern.

Year	Rank	Score
2002	36	9.5
2003	41	7.25
2004	46	10.5
2005	34	7.5
2006	32	8
2007	25	8.5
2008	47	9
2009	51	14
2010	65	18

Reporters Without Borders Press Freedom Index for Mauritius

For the sake of this paper, I will focus on the last decade starting with the report by Kenneth Morgan to the Media Trust on a proposed press council. It should here be noted that the Media Trust is an organisation which was created following the Media Trust Act which was enacted in 1994 and which is funded by the government with the stated aim of promoting the media mainly by providing training in the form of seminars, conferences, workshops and courses.

Unfortunately, the Media Trust is dysfunctional as the chairperson of the board has not been appointed by the government despite the fact that elections were held as scheduled to designate representatives of the press on the board in January 2006. These elected members thus resigned and the Media Trust has been almost inoperative since then.

First official proposal to self-regulate

The consultancy report which was commissioned by the Media Trust in 1998 under the chairmanship of Jean-Claude de l'Estrac examined the possibility of setting up a self-regulatory mechanism for

75

the local press. Morgan, a former director of the British Press Council and its successor, the Press Complaints Commission, then consultant to the Thomson

Foundation, chose to entitle his report "A Press Council for Mauritius?" with the subtitle "Safeguarding Freedom. Responsibility and Redress for Mauritius and its Media." The aim was to advocate self-regulation in the industry in order to preserve press freedom while addressing the grievances of Mauritian citizens against the local media. This was seen as a good means to curtail the need for more formal media laws. This endeavour is clearly confirmed by the statement which appears in the report that:

> *The detailed and tailored straitjacket of formal, special press laws may not be the best way of creating that machinery' (...) 'to offer judgement and redress to those who believe they are treated unfairly or unethically by the newspapers.*

Amongst persons consulted there was a quite large palette of media actors (from big media houses to smaller less known ones) as well as some non- state actors and politicians including government MPs and the opposition leader. Nearly all seemed to have been in favour of the proposal for a press council; only a small minority was against with one group advocating harsher laws and another rejecting any interference with the market forces. It should be noted here that one of the two main dailies' editor-in-chief who supported the latter views was not within the group of persons consulted.

In essence, Morgan's report proposed to set up a press council under the aegis of the existing Media Trust (thus with financial support from the government) or, if this failed, that the industry practitioners themselves take the initiative for a voluntary press council. The primary duty would have been "to preserve and defend press or media freedom as well as maintaining high professional and ethical standards and dealing with complaints." The Council would have had an equal number of representatives from the media (owners, editors and journalists) and from the public and be chaired by a "suitably qualified person otherwise unconnected with the press" and manned by a Director or Executive Secretary with experience of journalism at senior executive level. Although Morgan recommends that the suggested amendment in the Media Trust Act should not "deal in detail with the conduct or procedures of the press or media council," he suggests nonetheless that all procedures should be transparent and publicised to the public at large and that the first recourse should be towards mediation and conciliation rather than adjudication.

However, Morgan's proposal has not been implemented for lack of agreement within the media about the necessity and about the specific terms contained therein. It has often been said that the fact that the council would fall under the purview of the Media Trust Act and be dependent on government funds would jeopardise its independence and increase the risk of political interference. The possibility of a voluntary council seems to have been completely overlooked thus bringing the whole issue to a standstill. The government also did not seem to show any interest in exploring the recommendations put forward by the consultant.

Private media and the State

In the meantime, the long-standing debate about regulation of the media regularly crops up whenever the governing parties feel aggrieved by the coverage they receive in the private media. They thus regularly engage in public denunciations of the private media's alleged wrong doing (such as lack of objectivity, false news, defamation, etc.).

Over the last decade, there have indeed been regular threats from the government to impose stricter laws to regulate the media and these threats carry a name since the aftermath of the 2005 elections: the 'Media Commission Bill'. The sub-text of those regular statements is to punish the media for their alleged wrong-doing. The project of a Media Commission Bill with tougher media laws are even specifically referred to in the government programmes of 2005-2010 and 2010-2015.

Government Programme 2005-2010
Address by the President of the Republic

262. Government will amend the Independent Broadcasting Authority

Act to establish a Media Commission in lieu of the Independent Broadcasting Authority which will monitor and enforce legal provisions relating to the media in general.

Government Programme 2010-2015 Address by the President of the Republic

8. Government is committed to supporting the fundamental rights of all citizens, including privacy rights and freedom of expression. A plural, fair and independent media is an essential component of a democratic system. Accordingly, Government will introduce legislation for media law reform. Government will also support greater professionalism in the media and the powers and functions of the Independent Broadcasting Authority will be reviewed to provide for ethical conduct and safeguard of the fundamental rights of all our citizens.

In fact, government has been playing cat and mouse with the media, especially with the traditional private media, with a focus on *L'express* of La Sentinelle Group. The current PM and his ministers have regularly uttered harsh words against this newspaper in public meetings. In August 2006, *L'express* was publicly accused of being manipulated by the opposition party, the MMM (Mouvement Militant Mauricien). These accusations (added to the perennial ones about the private print media being dominated by the white and creole bourgeoisie) have served to justify the public pledges to bring about harsher media laws and a Media Commission. This has prompted a series of mutual attacks between the paper's editors and the members of government which have worsened over the next few years.

Incidentally, the members-to-be of the ruling coalition, the MSM party (Mouvement Socialiste Mauricien), had also engaged in the strife against the flagship title of La Sentinelle one year before elections and before becoming the official allies of the Labour Party. At that time, the paper had run some estimates of crowd attendance at an MSM political rally which angered the party. A group of rowdy partisans led by well-known figures of the party subsequently manifested in front of and broke some window panes at Radio One, a private radio station which is partly owned and managed by La Sentinelle.

During the same period, La Sentinelle chose to sue government over what it deems to be an inequitable distribution of government advertising expenditure at its expense. Its chairman publicly announced his resignation as president of the Empowerment Programme (a government funded programme designed to empower the poor). La Sentinelle also purports to be a victim of boycotts on the part of government, parastatal bodies as well as companies where the State is a majority shareholder. It should here be noted that the practice of cutting down on advertising to the newspapers perceived as enemies is not new. The leading weekly *Week-End* has been a 'victim' of this practice since 2005. But La Sentinelle was the first one to confront the government with a law suit on this issue.

The bitter relations between *L'express* and government cropped up especially during elections time in 2010 with an escalation of verbal confrontations through political meetings, media interviews and newspaper headlines. The interviews of the chairman of La Sentinelle, whereby he started making 'revelations' about the Prime Minister and the President of the country, have also no doubt helped fuel the press-government war with a particular focus on La Sentinelle and its flagship newspaper. To be fair, one should also recall that the current opposition party was also similarly dissatisfied with the media. Though it was under an MMM-MSM government that the airwaves were liberalised[35], the then prime minister Paul Bérenger often ranted against the private radio stations and threatened to ban live radio debates.

To date, the latest episode happened in November 2010 when the PM officially confirmed in Parliament that he had commissioned a report from Prof. Geoffrey Robertson QC for advice on the new media laws he wishes to introduce. The purpose being apparently to create a media commission to better regulate the local press.

Modest attempts at self-regulation

In response to these perceived attacks on the press, many in the private media have expressed the wish to self-regulate rather than to be submitted to State regulation but the attempts are so far quite modest. The proposal to self-regulate has in fact been the subject of hot debates between the two leading dailies of the country, L'express and Le Mauricien between 1999 and 2009, with the occasional publication of bitter editorials against each other.[36]

La Sentinelle was the first to launch a self-regulation initiative by setting up an internal mediation commission. This commission's mandate is to receive, investigate and provide conclusions on complaints made by members of the public in relation to its 'code de déontologie' (code of ethics) which was launched in October 2006. The committee is made up of a former judge, an academic and a well-known figure of the local press.

The code is available on the website of the daily newspaper[37]and it would seem that there are eight to ten cases which have been dealt

---

[35] The first private radio station, Radio One (a sister company of La Sentinelle) started airing in March 2002

[36] "Aurions-nous été des titres-voyous que, depuis longtemps déjà, les forces du marché auraient suffi pour nous renvoyer là où méritent de pâtir les voyous." - "Had we been rogue newspapers, the market forces would have sent us a long time ago to where rogues deserve to rot" Editorial by Gilbert Ahnee in Le Mauricien on 2nd July 2008.

[37]http://www.lexpress.mu/faq.pdf

with by the commission since its creation. Other newsrooms also claim to have their own code of ethics or conduct but these are not widely disseminated to the public and there is no evaluation with respect to their application.

The first industry move comes from the Newspapers Editors and Publishers Association (NEPA) which was set up in September 2006. It has set up a code of conduct in July 2010. The code has been produced by a committee comprising representatives of the following newspapers or media groups: Impact, Le Journal du Samedi, Business Publications, Le Défi Media Group, Le Mauricien and La Sentinelle. However, it is unclear what mechanisms are to be used to seek redress in case a journalist or newspaper belonging to the association is accused of not respecting the code.

As for the Association of Journalists, it has been moribund for the last four years despite a very enthusiastic start with the publication of a blog reporting on the meetings and discussions.

The way forward

Given this state of affairs, it is crucial to consider the way forward with sober objectivity. For one, regulation is of the essence. The form it takes is also of crucial importance. State regulation is helpful if the idea is to protect the interests of the public (not only of the elites) and its right to a private life, as well as to reduce or eliminate journalistic errors including publication of false news which can cause prejudice. However, we have to be careful about how State regulation is used or how the authorities threaten to use it. The frequent recourse to police questioning or threats of lawsuits are today tantamount to a form of intimidation against journalists.

On the one hand, leaving everything in the hands of the State is inevitably an open door to control by a single political party or coalition. Sooner or later, the ruling party will succumb to the temptation to censor, to manipulate or to indulge in propaganda, an immensely undesirable feature for any nation claiming to be a democracy. In fact, the absence of a Freedom of Information Act coupled with the very existence of archaic secrecy laws and regulations governing public offices are shameful pre- conditions which favour undemocratic tendencies. On the same note, the question of the current mode of nomination within existing regulating agencies is a cause for concern. Reform is here of the essence as noted in the 2008 African Media Barometer for Mauritius.

On the other hand, leaving everything to the market may encourage practices akin to collusion and thus irresponsible behaviour or to commoditisation of news and sensationalism. These shortcomings are already visible with the increasing tendency to give priority to 'hot' news related to crime, violence, sex and news having a commercial value coupled with frequent inaccuracies or gross over-simplification.

We definitely need reasonable doses of State regulation and industry self- regulation with an urgent necessity of giving more space for the people to participate in the democratic process. The media are the focus of so much attention because they are tied up with the very notion of democracy. Yet, we often forget that the word 'media' contains the idea of mediation, i.e. the media should act as a facilitator for the people to receive news of public interest.

This is why I tend to resent the expression 'fourth estate or power' as it suggests more control, more imposition on the people who are thus symbolically crushed (or 'interpellated' to use Althusser's term) by yet another institution (on top of schooling, work, religion, etc.). Likewise, the French term 'contre-pouvoir' (counter-power) makes me uneasy as it connotes the idea that the media should always be *against*, in other words, a thorn in the side of decision-makers, instead of being constructive.

I thus contend that the press should be able to inform as objectively as possible (though one can argue about the impossibility of achieving pure objectivity or neutrality but it is an ideal we aspire to), to shed light on wrong-doings as well as laudable initiatives. The threat of a Media Commission Bill should be considered as an excellent opportunity (rather than a threat) for the media to reinvent itself and reflect about the way it can better fulfil its watchdog function. The press should go through a continuous introspection and accept that its public has the right to criticise its content. It should also be committed to publicly admit its mistakes and be prepared to right any wrong done as far as possible. And if the press wants to reduce State regulation and the risk of political interference to a minimum, self-regulation seems the best course of action.

The pre-conditions for this are threefold:
• All media houses should agree on, adhere, and comply to the principles of self-regulation.
• Self-regulation should be done in a transparent manner. All deliberations and outcomes should be visible to the public.
• The process should be as inclusive of all stakeholder groups as possible and should include members of civil society as well as politicians.

The key question here is how to better serve the interests of the people who happen to rely on the news media to make informed decisions (for example about who to vote for). The audience should thus be central in this debate. They should be allowed to participate in the debate, to offer their views about the role of the media and in fact, to participate in the regulation process.

Indeed, as stated earlier by our Keynote speaker Amatou Mahtar Ba, we cannot leave regulation either in the sole hands of the State or in the sole hands of the media. And we cannot be content with mere lip service in the form of phantom codes of ethics.

Ideally, whatever regulating mechanism is adopted should make space for representatives of civil society, ordinary citizens who have no vested interest in either politics or the media business. Why? Simply because if the media err, the first victims are the members of the public who place their trust in the news media, not only by buying the papers or tuning in to the radio or television, but also by believing them and oftentimes actually participating in the circulation of the news content themselves.

In this context, the advent of interactive models of journalism which allow for dialogue, co-creation and scrutiny by readers/viewers is a sure sign that some form of self or co-regulation is already happening on online platforms. Media houses (as well as political actors) have to adapt to this new reality!

References

African Media Barometer for Mauritius, 2008, Friedrich Ebert Stiftung Foundation.

Althusser, L., 1969, Ideology and Ideological State Apparatuses (Notes towards an Investigation).

Government Programme 2005-2010.

Government Programme 2010-2015.

Habermas, J. (German 1962, English Translation 1989), The Structural Transformation of the Public Sphere: An Inquiry into a Category of Bourgeois Society, Thomas Burger, Cambridge Massachusetts: The MIT Press.

La Sentinelle: Code de Déontologie, 2006.

Morgan, K., 1998-99, A Press Council for Mauritius? Consultancy Report OBE for the Media Trust.

Newspapers Editors and Publishers Association (NEPA): Code of Conduct, 2010.

Reporters Without Borders, Press Freedom Indices for 2002 to 2010.

Simonin, J., 2005, "Media and democracy in the islands in the Indian Ocean. Transnational research and typological perspective. Regional Conference: *Media and democracy in an age of transition*, (17-18 May, Mauritius, OSSREA Mauritius chapter), pp. 66-89.

11

Mainstream Political Parties and the Media

Hon. Cehl Fakeemeah,
Leader of FSM

It is a pleasure for me to be associated with this important and timely event especially when the role of the media is being questioned. I will try to bring my humble contribution to the event through my presentation. I would like to seize the opportunity to thank all the persons at UOM and UNESCO who have initiated and organized the event.

The right for information and the freedom of expression are two fundamentals of democracy. Undue control of these fundamentals is tantamount to perversion of democracy paving the way to a totalitarian system or even dictatorship. In these latter systems the strength of the government resides in the ignorance of the masses.

In Mauritius, the media and the political parties have always shared a relationship of complicity. By the time of Independence, the newspapers such as *Advance* and *Le Cernéen* had divergent views on independence and supported the political motives of political parties, directly or indirectly. The two mainstream political parties of that time were the Labour Party and the PMSD (Parti Mauricien Social Démocrate). After the independence, the MMM gained momentum by the early 1970's with the support of their own newspaper *Le Militant*. The 1980's witnessed the emergence of the MSM (Mouvement Socialiste Mauricien) supported by *The Sun*, their own newspaper. The 1990's witnessed the emergence and evolution of the FSM (Front Socialiste Mauricien) without any newspaper of its own and without any other newspaper or other form of media support.

Today with the advent of electronic media, most mainstream political parties do not possess their own newspaper, except for the MMM (Mouvement Militant Mauricien) with *Le Militant* which is itself going on- line, but they do have an indirect influence on part of the media. Many journalists act in favour of a political party. The perception in Mauritius today is that media players do have marked political affinities.

The international trend today is the use of social networks like Facebook, the use of Twitter and blogs. President Obama's election was due to a large extent to Facebook. We have also witnessed the use of these networks in the last general elections in 2010 in Mauritius.

Today the relationship between the government and the press is confrontational. The former is accusing the latter of being biased and not so called independent. Let us be frank. There cannot be a totally neutral press as journalists like any other person have inclinations. Also we cannot ask the press to be only factual and not to make any analysis or criticism. This is against the democratic fundamental of freedom of expression. Should a person feel that he or she is being wrongly targeted, he or she can have recourse to a court of justice.

But then why does the government not set the example by making the MBC truly neutral and independent by selecting a media professional as director through open recruitment instead of political nomination? There cannot be true democracy in Mauritius until and unless the government stops MBC monopoly and liberalises local TV services and puts in place an Independent Broadcasting Authority not headed by a political nominee. Big democracies such as India and the UK have liberalised their audio visual industry. Luckily the radio services have been liberalised, so at least the masses have a platform to express themselves. The radio stations are in fact doing a wonderful job.

Though it tries to maintain a neutral image, the Mauritius Broadcasting Corporation (MBC) has always been the communication arm of the government of the day. During election time this year, the outgoing government used it as a tool for propaganda. There is a perception that it manages public opinion in its favour, thus disadvantaging the other political parties. This, along with uncontrolled excessive funding and expenses by major political parties during elections (note that there is no law for controlling funding of political parties), renders the democratic process of elections unfree and unfair.

La désinformation est une manipulation de l'opinion publique, à des fins politiques, avec une information traitée par des moyens détournés. Il s'agit d'un procédé de conditionnement des esprits s'adressant à des populations entières. Notre démocratie fait face à la désinformation à notre époque. On voit des régimes dits démocratiques où l'opinion publique et la volonté générale sont censées faire la loi. Il est fatal que la désinformation, procédé de manipulation de l'opinion, joue un rôle de premier plan et soit financée par le gros capital à leur profit. C'est cette désinformation que nous dénonçons aujourd'hui dans ce forum.

The emergence and ascension of the FSM party has been made possible even without having its own press or the support of the press or other forms of media. Though the FSM supports freedom of expression, it has itself been regularly marginalised by the press. The press could not understand its ideology and even made negative propaganda and a "trial by the press" of its leader. The question then is: How did FSM manage to survive and sustain its growth over a span of twenty years? How has it managed to become a national mainstream political party and eventually a determining party in local politics?

The philosophy of the FSM is based on national solidarity, caring and compassion for the poor and true meritocracy and justice for all. The FSM has set up and consolidated a strong social network in the country and practices a politicy of truth and proximity. Its leader is present quasi permanently for solicitations and never makes false promises and always keeps his words. He practices an open door policy. All his actions are communicated through the social network and over the years people have known him closely and hence have developed a trust in him and the FSM. That is why negative propaganda has been ineffective and has given FSM three historic victories:

1. In 1996 when for the first time two FSM candidates were elected for the municipal elections in Port-Louis.
2. In 2001, when the leader of the FSM was elected while being unjustly put behind bars.
3. The election of its leader in the last general elections held in 2010.

Today the FSM is using the electronic media (Facebook, websites) to reach out to its adherents and the population.

Conclusion and Recommendations

1. For a healthy democracy it is important to have divergent media in Mauritius. There should not be a *"pensée unique."* This is dangerous for democracy.
2. People are not wholly influenced by the media, there are other issues which are taken into consideration for political decisions.
3. Party-owned press is losing significance.
4. Electronic media is the new force of political parties.
5. We must legislate in favour of a responsible media and sanction the media in case of false news and disinformation.
6. We must establish an impartial Independent Broadcasting Authority without political nominees.
7. We must liberalise the audio visual sector and stop the MBC monopoly.

12

Partis Politiques et Médias

Hon. Steven Obeegadoo
Porte -Parole du MMM

Le texte qui suit est une transcription faite à partir d'un enregistrement audio de l'intervenant.

I wish to first point out that this is a laudable initiative on the part of the University of Mauritius. I must commend the University for taking such a proactive role at a time when indeed the subject of politics, media and democracy is central to public debate.

It is in fact the first time that I am being invited as member of the Opposition party to the University of Mauritius. I have been previously invited when I was a Minister but not when I was in the Opposition. It may be a sign that times are changing.

Also, I am happy to see that all newspapers including L'express are available today for collection in this Lecture Theatre. Even my colleague from parliament1 has taken her copy of L'express!

Le contexte

Comme mentionné plus haut, cette initiative intervient à un moment où la relation entre la presse, la démocratie et la politique est au centre du débat public.

Nous sommes dans un contexte des dernières élections générales où l'Opposition actuelle officielle a dénoncé, toute la campagne durant, le rôle malsain joué par la radio télévision nationale. L'Opposition continue d'ailleurs à dire que les résultats ont été faussés par la télévision nationale.

C'est aussi le contexte de la contestation de l'instance régulatrice dont parlait tout à l'heure Mme Meetoo. Nous savons tous qu'au sein de la presse, de l'opposition et des forces citoyennes, la légitimité de cette instance régulatrice est contestée en raison de sa composition.

C'est aussi le contexte de la guerre ouverte entre l'État et un grand groupe de presse en particulier. Guerre permanente avec chaque jour son lot de menaces et de répliques.

Enfin, contexte depuis de longs mois, de l'arrestation arbitraire de journalistes de divers groupes de presse. Un traitement véritablement indigne où les journalistes sont traités comme de vulgaires malfrats, escortés par des policiers au tribunal pour déposer une caution!

En somme, contexte malheureux mais approprié et propice pour un tel débat.

Principes généraux

Je vais ici présenter la position du MMM, rappeler nos principes par rapport à la question de la presse, de la démocratie et de la politique, nos engagements passés et présents en faveur de la liberté de la presse et nos propositions pour une autre île Maurice.

Prenons comme point de départ la déclaration universelle des droits de l'homme. Toute l'humanité s'est inscrite en faveur de normes universelles régissant les sociétés nationales et internationales. Cette déclaration s'intéresse à la liberté d'opinion et d'expression et la liberté de chercher, de recevoir, de répandre les informations. Liberté d'informer... liberté de la presse.

Je veux également faire référence à la déclaration de Brisbane – la liberté d'information qui correspond au droit de savoir est essentielle à la démocratie et aux droits de l'homme. Le droit à l'information fait partie intégrante de la liberté d'expression. La liberté de la presse est en fait une condition préalable à l'exercice des droits de l'être humain et l'exercice des libertés fondamentales.

En somme, le droit à l'information concerne la démocratie et la gouvernance: prises de décision éclairées, participation à la vie démocratique, contrôle de l'action publique, renforcement de la transparence, obligation de rendre des comptes et lutte contre la corruption.

Il est à souligner que, demain, c'est la notion des sociétés du savoir qui importera le plus, des sociétés inclusives comme souhaitées par l'Unesco où la liberté d'expression et l'accès universel à l'information sont essentielles.

Aussi, le recours aux technologies de l'information et de la communication (les TIC) et la révolution de l'internet facilitent le droit de l'information pour tous. D'ailleurs, nombre de jeunes Mauriciens ont déjà recours à l'internet pour s'informer.

Le droit d'opinion et la liberté de la presse qui est fondamentale à l'exercice des droits démocratiques sont des facteurs primordiaux de développement économique et social.

Les engagements du MMM

Notre déclaration de principe de 1998 s'exprime contre les monopoles et en faveur de la pluralité et de la libéralisation des ondes tout en veillant à la protection du tissu social fragile de Maurice et finalement une prise de position contre les implications du regroupement des capitaux. Nous ne sommes pas contre le regroupement des capitaux mais demeurons vigilants sur les implications par rapport à la pluralité de la presse.

Je me plais toujours à rappeler cette citation de Rosa Luxembourg figurant dans notre programme de 1976: « La liberté c'est toujours la liberté de celui qui pense autrement ."

Je rappellerai notre combat contre la censure dans les années 1970-71, notre combat contre le renvoi des élections législatives en 1972 et des élections municipales en 1977. Puis au gouvernement, les amendements constitutionnels pour rendre impossible le renvoi des élections. Le combat aussi du début des années 1980 associé à Vikramsing Ramlallah, Sir Kher Jagatsing, Jean Claude de l'Estrac et soutenu par le MMM concernant le dépôt à être fourni par ceux qui voulaient lancer de nouveaux titres. Enfin, la dépolitisation de la MBC: la seule et unique fois où le directeur de la MBC fut recruté à partir d'un appel public dans la période 2000-2005 et évidemment le lancement des radios privées.

Or, il y a quatre éléments fondamentaux pour l'avenir:

1. Un État respectueux de la presse. La relation État-presse est toujours difficile et complexe et souvent nécessairement conflictuelle. Pourtant la presse est un contre-pouvoir essentiel. Quand j'étais ministre, j'étais moi-même souvent exaspéré. Mais la presse aura été très utile de par ses critiques lors de l'action gouvernementale que j'avais menée. Il s'agit d'un rôle fondamental pour éviter les dérives, pour nous rappeler les préoccupations quotidiennes de monsieur-tout-le- monde.

Il y a nécessité de définir des instances de dialogues au lieu d'insultes, de menaces. Il faut y avoir des dialogues. L'association de la presse (directeurs et rédacteurs en chef) doit s'asseoir avec l'État pour définir les instances de dialogue, rétablir la légitimité des instances de régulation de par leur composition et le respect et la protection des journalistes dans l'exercice de leur fonction.

2. Pour une presse professionnelle et responsable. La note conceptuelle parle de *'unfettered'* (sans entraves), indépendante, ce qui ne veut pas dire pas lié à un parti politique. Le MMM a toujours eu son organe de presse qui ne reçoit aucune directive pour sa ligne éditoriale. Une presse objective, ce qui ne veut pas dire impartiale, mais plutôt un souci de l'objectivité.

Il faut former, pas juste les journalistes mais tous ceux concernés par l'information, ceux qui sont dans la régulation et l'auto-régulation. Je lance d'ailleurs un appel au gouvernement: il faut voir ce qui se fait dans les grandes démocraties, par exemple en France, plutôt que de menacer.

Il faut venir avec un *'white paper'* (livre blanc) explicitant ce que propose le gouvernement et le soumettre à un débat public et non pas utiliser chaque sortie publique pour insulter et menacer la presse. Et la presse doit faire aussi preuve de responsabilité, ce qu'elle fait de manière générale.

3. Libérer l'audiovisuel. Il est inconcevable qu'il y ait toujours un monopole d'État sur la télévision dans une démocratie. Il faut de la diversité. Nous prônons un financement adéquat des chaînes publiques et un cahier des charges pour le privé pour une compétition féconde. Il faut aussi la fin de l'ingérence politique à la MBC et la formation- professionnalisation et *l'empowerment* de la MBC.

4. Enfin, gare au monopole. On n'en parle pas suffisamment. Il faut une presse aux couleurs de Maurice. Il est concevable que demain des groupes étrangers (multinationales de l'information) deviennent propriétaires de tous les grands titres de presse à Maurice.

Il nous faut une presse respectueuse de la diversité de la société mauricienne qui est traversée par des courants d'opinion différents: sur la peine de mort, sur la légalisation du cannabis (gandia), sur l'avortement. La presse doit être respectueuse et refléter cette diversité. Une presse démocratique se doit d'être le reflet des idéologies souvent conflictuelles au sein de la société, qui est une société diverse avec des classes sociales, avec des visions différentes. La presse, pour être vraiment démocratique, ne peut être prisonnière du pouvoir de l'argent, ne peut être sujet au monopole.

En ce moment il y a une atmosphère très lourde et pesante de par ce conflit au quotidien entre l'État et un grand groupe de presse. Cela est mauvais pour la démocratie, ce n'est pas propice pour l'avancement du pays. Il y a tellement de questions internationales et nationales qui requièrent notre attention que l'on ne peut focaliser toute la vie nationale sur le conflit État versus un grand groupe de presse au quotidien.

Je fais un appel à ceux qui nous gouvernent pour dire halte aux invectives et de dire clairement ce que souhaite le gouvernement, de dialoguer avec les représentants de la presse pour trouver une solution à ce qui trouble le gouvernement et avancer. S'il le faut, revoir le cadre légal, s'inspirer des grandes démocraties et le rendre public.

J'en appelle aussi aux responsables de la presse: la presse doit être prête à un tel dialogue pour sortir de l'impasse et avancer dans la démocratisation de notre société. Il nous faut promouvoir la relation entre la presse, la démocratie et la politique.

13

Mainstream Political Parties and the Media

Hon. Nita Deerpalsing
Spokesperson for Labour Party

The following text was transcribed from an audio recording of the speaker.

Thank you for organising this two-day conference. I come here with a lot of interest, not only because I am here to represent the Mauritius Labour Party but also because I am personally interested in the media.

I have to openly state my biases and my influences. A lot of my thinking about the media has been influenced by the writings of Noam Chomsky and Edward Herman inter alia.

I have spent a lot of my time when I was not in Mauritius studying the structure of the media and have been influenced by the perspectives of those two thinkers as to how the media operates and what it can do and cannot do.

La perspective de Chomsky sur l'utilisation des médias aux États-Unis est essentielle à tous les étudiants en Communication. Deux livres doivent ici être cités notamment, 'Necessary Illusions. Thought Control in Democratic Societies' et 'Manufacturing Consent. The Political Economy of the Media'.

Même si cette lecture n'est pas nécessairement transposable au contexte mauricien, certaines analyses sont tout de même pertinentes.

John Lloyd's book – 'What the Media are doing to our Politics' offers a pertinent analysis on the power of the media to shape and bend contemporary politics.

I am very happy about this dialogue session because I think that politicians, whether they are from the opposition or the majority side, have to be part of the debate as they represent the people whose freedom the media claim they are **in the business** (and I stress) to protect. The key element however, beside the politicians and the media, is civil society. It is the network of public actors, public opinion and independent political activists (which are unfortunately rare in this country) which must determine how society reflects itself to itself.

I quote from Chomsky's book:

"Information from sources is likely to be partial, self-interested for one reason or the other on the part of the source and often at the service of a point rather than accuracy. That is the source has his or her own case to make and is using the media to do it. Sometimes, the more willing the source is to give information the less reliable it is because the motive might not be the right one."

Mrs Chan-Meetoo talked about regulation earlier. Regulation can only give a framework within which the stakeholders operate. The culture of the media can only be created and constantly renewed by those who work in them and those who are concerned with the work.

We are not here referring to politicians from the government but to all politicians. Unfortunately, and this is not specific to Mauritius, politicians are always thought to be 'rotten'. The posture of most of the media, not just in Mauritius but across the world, whether in Canada or the United States, in United Kingdom or France, is that politics is a degraded profession. Probably a fair part of it is true but within every profession, there are rotten apples including politicians.

Concerning the tension between the media and politics, I am pleased that previous presenters have mentioned that the tension which exists between one media group (La Sentinelle) and government concerns one media group only and not the media as a whole. The struggle between politicians and the media is critical because this conflict, as mentioned by Honourable

Obeegadoo is usually represented as a heavy clash of independent institutions in a democratic space. However, sometimes this assumes the character of a zero-sum game struggle for power.

> *Je dois dire ici que je porte plusieurs chapeaux. Je parle au nom de mon parti mais aussi en mon nom personnel. Mon avis personnel est que ce conflit est justement un 'zero-sum game struggle for power' – for who has the last word.*
>
> *Bien sûr ce n'est pas toujours le cas. Parfois il y a collusion entre les politiciens même de la majorité ou de l'opposition et les médias. Je vous donne un exemple concret. En 2006, il y a eu une bataille extrêmement importante au sujet de la réforme de l'industrie sucrière. Mr Subron pourra en parler plus tard.*
>
> *Où se positionnait le groupe La Sentinelle par rapport à ce débat? Et l'opposition? Et même (je le dis sans gêne) un Ministre de l'ancien gouvernement? Where was the balance of power?*

Anyway, this tension between politics, power and the media is not healthy because it diminishes rather than enhances freedom and it causes greater fragmentation within civil society. Many in the media dislike this argument because it strikes at the heart both of their idealistic self-belief and their everyday practices and use of power.

À la fin de la journée, un groupe de presse c'est quoi? C'est un business, une entité corporate. Which exists to make profits. The concept note of this conference refers to unfettered, independent and objective media. But I say this is a myth; there is no such thing as unfettered, independent and objective media. There can be neutrality and balanced views which is different.

> *Un groupe de presse, c'est un business qui est là pour faire des profits en premier lieu. L'audience, c'est des consommateurs qui achètent.*

By the way, I find the argument that people go to vote every day very idiotic. When people go and buy cigarettes every day, they don't go to vote every day. There is a sociological need to buy papers since the advent of print media. People don't go and vote to kill themselves when they go and buy cigarettes every day. So the question we have to ask is: what is the institutional structure of the media? How is it organised? How is it controlled? This is what Chomsky asks all the time. How is it funded? What is the relationship between media groups and the banks in this country? Can La Sentinelle ever publish anything against the Mauritius Commercial Bank? These are important questions. I would appreciate if someone could furrow in the archives to see whether La Sentinelle has ever published critical stories against the MCB.

In conclusion, there are different perspectives. When we are in an intellectual space like this, we should not limit ourselves to propaganda - whether it is from a political party or from the media or any self-interest based organisation. We should be able to weigh all the perspectives. Let our minds be washed with all these perspectives so as to be able to draw our very own conclusions.

14

Interactive session with mainstream political parties

The following text was transcribed from an audio recording of the session.

1. Question to Hon. S. Obeegadoo: Would you pledge if you were elected in the next election to change the mode of nomination of members of the MBC or the regulatory bodies?

Hon. S. Obeegadoo: Yes, we shall be revisiting the whole manner of appointment of those responsible of the MBC but also the IBA should be revisited in the manner of appointing members so that these institutions have credibility and there is consensus within society that they are above party politics.

Let me put a question: is there one single society regarded as a democracy where there is state monopoly over television? There is not one. Mauritius cannot claim it is a democracy as long as it has state monopoly over the MBC, which is biased and partisan and even those in government recognise it and their argument is that it has to be so because the media, the written press is controlled by 'the others'. But there is no truth in that, those who have followed the written press for the last 20-30 years can testify to the fact that today there is not one single group which controls the whole market.

Many new newspapers have emerged: *Le Défi, Le Matinal,* so many others. Private radio stations have also emerged controlled by different groups, there is no longer any monopoly. Today the majority of Mauritians (60% or more) watch the MBC news as their main if not their sole source of information, hardly more than a third rely on the newspapers for their information, so you can judge the impact state monopoly over a biased and unashamedly partisan television broadcasting service can have. Mauritius cannot be considered a democracy as this continues.

2. Question addressed to both Ms Deerpalsing and Mr Obeegadoo: It is easy to say many things especially when in opposition and make rhetorical promises. Be more concrete than just words. What can you tell us today beyond mere words? The street grumbles, the blogosphere is wilder.

Hon. N. Deerpalsing: I am here to represent the Mauritius Labour Party not the government as I am not part of the executive. My views about the MBC have been aired in various interviews in the media and I not have minced my words about how the MBC has paid disservice to the government.

Je dois faire ressortir que jamais on n'entend les parlementaires de l'opposition critiquer le gouvernement en place quand ils sont dans le camp de la majorité gouvernementale. Pas autant que vous le voyez aujourd'hui que le Parti Travailliste est au pouvoir. Et c'est souvent exploité par les médias pour dire qu'il y a du désordre au sein du parti. C'est un mythe de dire qu'un parti politique est monolithique. En tout cas, ce n'est pas le cas au Parti Travailliste. Il y a vraiment des débats, parfois houleux.

Au parti, nous aurions souhaité une libéralisation. D'ailleurs la loi pour la libéralisation des ondes a été votée en 2000 avant l'arrivée du gouvernement MMM-MSM. Il faut mettre des 'counter-checks' même s'il y a la loi.

The big question: is who funds media? If it is dominant banks, this is not democracy.

Hon. S. Obeegadoo: Ms Deepalsing is wrong to say she is not part of the executive - she receives a salary and an allowance as deputy director of the "Democratisation of the Economy Commission' which does not come from the budget of the National Assembly. My second point: Ms Deepalsing alleged that I spoke of the conflict between the state and one press group.

This is not true, the repression against the press has meant the police arrest of people from *L'express*, *Le Défi*, journalists from *Radio One* and *Le Militant* - not one press group alone.

In the latest incident, a minister uttered certain words not fitting democracy and was reported on another radio not belonging to La Sentinelle and conveniently everything comes back to media bashing against one group. We are concerned with respecting the freedom of expression for all journalists and all media groups.

The proof of pudding is in the eating. The Freedom of Information Act - who spoke about that? In the 1990's the Labour Party talked about it – nothing happened, there was no commitment from the Labour Party to reform the MBC in its manifesto.

Who in practice liberalised radio in Mauritius? It was the last government of the MMM and the MSM. It was a tricky exercise but it has revolutionised the media in Mauritius and it was a step by step approach. Our approach at the MMM is to have an independent person recruited to head the MBC though Ashok Subron said it did not make much difference. Of course we need to go much further and the MMM is willing to take any commitment whatsoever to liberalise the air waves having regard to television the moment we come back to government and if UOM wants a declaration with a written commitment by political parties, the MMM is ready to sign an official legal written commitment to the university. The MMM will be first to sign.

Questions to Hon. N. Deerpalsing

1. Do you have any information about the Media Commission Bill? When will this happen?

Hon. N. Deerpalsing: I have no information about the Media Commission Bill but I think it will be sooner rather than later. The need is becoming more and more acute for the professionalization of the journalistic trade. In all professions, accountability is necessary and it is necessary to have good people as well.

There are legal means of course but they are not sufficient as there is too much false news. [The speaker explains in detail a brief article that apparently insinuated that she had distributed fruits coming from an Islamic Centre during the Eid festival.]

And I agree that the Media Commission has to be open to public debate. Other press groups have been involved in arrests but the context today after general elections is with La Sentinelle.

Le gouvernement ou la majorité gouvernementale ne s'attend pas à la complaisance ou la flatterie de n'importe quel type de presse. D'autres médias tels que le Week-End et le Défi nous critiquent également. Par exemple, Radio Plus a diffusé les propos du ministre Choonee. Mais la goutte d'eau qui a fait déborder le vase c'est quand la Sentinelle a publié un article sur les castes. La tension est entre le gouvernement et la Sentinelle parce que celle-ci en a trop fait. Il y a au moins une dizaine d'articles complètement faux.

Criticism is good to uncover the rot but publication of false news is unacceptable. La Sentinelle indulges in false publication.

I would also be interested to know if it is acceptable for a journalist who is absent from an event to write about the event at length. This is a common practice at La Sentinelle for journalists to sign an article in which they cite me verbatim and those journalists were never present. I often have to send audio recordings to chief editors to redress. Is this professional?

As for electoral promises, politicians have justifiable aspirations for the country but whether they can deliver or do deliver is another thing. And the people will ultimately judge whether they have delivered or whether the intention to do so is there.

15

Extra-parliamentary Dynamics and the Media

Ashok Subron
Spokesperson for Rezistans ek Alternativ

The following text was transcribed from an audio recording of the speaker.

It is quite interesting, after listening to the two mainstream parties to see that they are competing to quote leftist and even Marxists thinkers like Chomsky or Rosa Luxemburg. Some people thought that radical left philosophy no more stands good in political debates. But it is reassuring to hear the contrary!

Rezistans ek Alternativ as you know acts as an extra parliamentary political movement. And the invitation today is a recognition of extra parliamentary forces as an agent and as a subject of societal change. Changes and transformations in society have never been and can never be confined within the existing and dominant power structure of any society. Extra parliamentary forces include broadly: political forces, social forces, people and citizen movements operating outside the formal structure of power.

Historically, parliament itself is a product of extra parliamentary political action and forces. In Mauritius in particular during colonial times, extra parliamentary forces have challenged the parliamentary colonial rule. During the 70's with the birth of the MMM, which was itself an extra parliamentary force it was so powerful that the media itself had to be stifled and muffled and repressed because of the ascendancy of this movement in the 70's.

During the past 20 years, extra parliamentary forces have mainly consisted of the leftist forces because they have a coherent and sustained political progamme and alternative. I would say that political expression and social movement outside parliament are also vital for a democratic state just as the parliament and the media are crucial and critical for a real democracy.

But one should note that in a more liberal, caplitalist and class based society, the media has a dual characteristic. It is the vehicle and the means of the freedom of expression, of opinion and of information. But within a particular society which is class based and market based the media is itself embedded within class and social conflict dynamics. This is an objective fact because of the inequality of distribution of power in society - one media tends to present reality in a particular fashion.

In Mauritius, the media has also been influenced by 3 factors:

1. The history of the written press itself which exists since 1875. The written press was born out of a deal to abolish slavery. Despite this fact, there has been a long, a very rich history of the wrtiten press in Mauritius.

2. What happened during the independence period: the communalist

vibes and the communal riots, have also influenced the press in a positive way I would say.

3. In the post-independence period in the 1970's, the state of

emergency and the censorship of the press have shaped what we have as media with all its contradictions.

One has to recognise that extra parliamentary movements do have a fair representation within the commercial media. During the last 15-20 years, many people including the intelligentsia and people from the press realized that there are some disturbing features about Mauritian politics and this includes the press too. There is a kind of recognition of the corruption of democracy and of the democratic process, which can even be termed « a Failed Democracy ». On the one hand, we have big money *('bailleurs de fond')* running electoral campaigns and on the other hand, we have communalist lobbies running and determining more and more what kind of political campaign we will have and the kind of party coalition we will have on the eve of elections. People in the media themselves have recognised this corruption of democracy.

And the media itself is influenced by corporate interests; there is a big dependency on advertising. We also have the state controlled media which is very much soviet style control. We just have to turn on our TV to see that. But it should be noted that there is no monopoly of this kind of state control. It was like this even when there was an independent person directing the MBC TV. There was no fundamental difference in the state's control of public television.

Let me now focus on the actions of Rezistans ek Alternativ.

Rezistans ek Alternativ is a leftist political movement which believes in the transformation of democracy itself. The type of democracy we have is very limited and we have to move towards a more participatory form of democracy. We have been focusing during the past four years on challenging at least one of the components in terms of corrupting democracy in Mauritius, i.e. communalism within the political structure and the structure of power itself. During elections, we have stood candidate without mentioning any communal affiliation. This has been an extra parliamentary action in itself expressing a form of alternative politics

This has shown that extra parliamentary forces who wish to participate in the democratic process of the country cannot do so without defining themselves communally. This has exposed a very important contradiction of the Mauritian democracy. Equally important: this action has acted and continues to act as a catalyst to trigger electoral reforms. Many in the media, the intelligentsia and democratic people are calling for an electoral and a consitutional reform but most are trapped in the system. The action of Rezistans ek Alternativ on the political front and legal front is giving space and acting as catalyst and driver for reform. The media have recognised this fact which is why they give us fair and reasonable space.

107

I will conclude by saying that the extra parliamentary forces are as important as the media itself in a free and democratic society. There is almost a diametrical relation between the media and the extra parliamentary forces. The media is as critical for the expression of the extra parliamentary forces as extra parliamentary forces are critical to ensure the total independence of the media from the state, from corporate or market based interests or religious interests.

The march towards a free society is one where the media reflects citizens' reality and the media should be under the scrutiny of citizens, not the state. İt should not be biasedly self-regulated. We should have a system where there is citizen regulation. I think that it is mainly technological innovations which might offer this possibility for the media not to be entirely under the control of corporate interests or state monopoly. We have to think about the pertinence of using new forms of technology to bring in citizen participation and reader participation. This is in fact the political objective of Rezistans ek Alternativ.

16

Extra-parliamentary Dynamics and the Media

Nilen Vencadasamy
Barrister-at-Law, Member of Blok 104

First and foremost, allow me to thank the organising committee of this session for having invited 'Blok 104' to be part of today's panel and to address you on "Extra-parliamentary Dynamics and the Media."

'Blok 104' was born following the Nomination Day of the General Election which was held earlier this year[38]. Let me hasten to say that we do not consider ourselves, at least at this stage, as a political party, nor as a political player, but simply a group of citizens, endeared to republican values, and who firmly believe in a secular, egalitarian Republic, devoid of any communal consideration.

On the 17 March of this year, which was the Nomination Day for the 2010 general election, we were a number of citizens of this Republic who felt compelled by the struggle embarked upon by Rezistans ek Alternativ since 2005.

44 citizens from all walks of our society, workers, students, artists, professionals, responded to the plea of Rezistans ek Alternativ and Muvman 1er Mai, which had formed a common political platform, fielding

60 candidates in 20 constituencies, and together, 104 Mauritians stood up to challenge communal classifications, entrenched within our Constitution and our electoral process ever since we achieved our independence.

Thus 104 out of some 550 candidates, representing some 16% of total candidacies, had refused to state, in their nomination papers, to

---

[38] Year 2010

which community they belonged, whether Hindu, Muslim, Sino-Mauritian or General Population, a constitutional and statutory prerequisite for the validity of one's candidacy to a general election in Mauritius.

The resulting invalidation of our candidacies led to judicial proceedings, the legal intricacies of which I shall not allude to, which are still pending before the Judicial Committee of the Privy Council, the highest judicial authority for Mauritius.

In as much as we wanted to help perpetuate the fight against communalism, those of us, commonly referred to as "independent candidates" who had together with members of the 'Platform Pou Enn Nouvo Konstitisyon', frontally challenged the communal classification within our electoral process, decided to regroup.

Interestingly enough it is the former Editor-in-Chief of *L'express Dimanche,* now regular columnist for the weekly, Nad Sivaramen, who first coined the name 'Blok 104'.

In one of his columns following the Nomination Day, Mr. Sivaramen had this to say:

« Faisons comme la presse ailleurs, et prenons ouvertement position pour un bloc en vue du scrutin du 5 mai. Nous optons pour le bloc 104 pour le symbole d'ouverture qu'il incarne ! »

That is to say that, in a way, 'Blok 104', which is how our group of citizens has come to be known thereafter, owes its very existence to the media.

Political parties like Rezistans ek Alternativ or groups like 'Blok 104' may have the most laudable ideas, engage in the most commendable course of action and struggle; the undeniable fact remains that with our limited means, it would be virtually impossible to reach a majority of Mauritians without the help of the media.

And we, more than anybody else, rely heavily on the traditional print and broadcast press to disseminate our ideas and convey our message.

While journalists are being regularly jailed and persecuted in certain regions of the world for daring to challenge those in power...While restrictive media laws in many countries are threatening to curtail freedom of expression guaranteed by these countries' constitutions, or by international conventions to which these very countries have adhered to... While Government control of print and broadcast media in many other countries leave little scope for dissenting opinions and, therefore, public debate...We in Mauritius, save perhaps for our national broadcaster, can boast a really free press.

A press which gives the opportunity to one and all to voice out their opinions - that is precisely why groups of citizens like 'Blok 104' with their more than limited means have been able to exist within the Mauritian media space.

In any democracy, the prime role of the press is to allow access to information. Democracy requires the active participation of citizens and ideally, the media should keep citizens engaged in the business of governance by informing, educating and mobilising the public.

The media ensures that citizens make responsible, informed choices rather than acting out of ignorance or misinformation. The information exchanged serves as a "checking function" by ensuring that elected representatives uphold their oaths of office, electoral promises and carry out the wishes of those who elected them.

This is precisely why the media is referred to as the Fourth Estate within a democracy. Contemporary democratic theory appreciates the media's role in ensuring governments are held accountable. In both new and old democracies, the notion of the media as watchdog and not merely a passive recorder of events is widely accepted. Governments, it is argued, cannot be held accountable if citizens are ill informed about the actions of officials and institutions. The watchdog press is guardian of the public interest.

This is precisely why freedom of expression is a consecrated right within our Constitution and Constitutions of many other countries, as well as a number of international human rights instruments. The media provides voice to those marginalized because of poverty, gender, or ethnic or religious affiliation. By giving these groups a

111

place in the media, their views – and their afflictions – become part of mainstream public debate and hopefully contribute to a social consensus that the injustices against them ought to be redressed. In this way, the media also contribute to the easing of social conflicts and to promoting reconciliation among divergent social groups.

The achievement of Rezistans ek Alternativ and 'Blok 104' in the context of the recent general election has undoubtedly been, through our action, to have restored a true *debat d'idée* in an otherwise insipid political campaign, to have sparked a profound reflection amongst the population not only on the flaws of our electoral process and political system but on the emergence of a nation, or rather what is preventing such an emergence.

And we have been able to achieve this only because the press has in its vast majority provided an extensive coverage to our every move thus making our recriminations against communal classifications within our electoral system, part of the mainstream public debate, to such an extent that even the MBC TV and Radio had no alternative than to give coverage to the judicial proceedings to which we were privy, even covering our regular press conferences. Such is the power of a free, independent press.

This is precisely why any attempt to curtail the liberty of the press is purely and simply unacceptable and any attempt to impose government sponsored regulatory bodies is utterly intolerable; the more so when protective provisions, such as defamation laws and remedies, exist and are readily available to one and all.

This is precisely why modern Mauritius can no more condone the abject servility to which our national television and radio station is subjected vis- à-vis the government of the day.

In fact, an antagonistic relationship between media and government is almost desirable and represents a vital and healthy element of fully functioning democracies.

In this respect, it may be apposite for some political leaders to ponder on this celebrated declaration attributed to Thomas Jefferson, who, for all his bitterness against journalistic criticism, had this to say:

"Were it left to me to decide whether we should have a government without newspapers or newspapers without government, I should not hesitate to prefer the latter."

Thank you for your attention

17

The Media and Free & Fair Elections

Mayila Paroomal
Senior Lecturer at University of Mauritius

The first part of this paper looks at the role of the media in free & fair elections, the second part identifies the conditions necessary for the media to fulfil their role, and the third part makes a case for media monitoring around elections.

1) Free and fair elections: the role of the media

Free and Fair Elections: A relatively new concept in the democratic process

For many today, elections are the hallmarks of a democratic political system (Elklit and Svensson, 1997). But it is only in the past two to three decades that democracy has known a significant global expansion, which has in turn led to an extraordinary focus on the institution of elections. Consequently, "free and fair" has become universally recognized as the standard by which the quality of elections is to be judged.

However, references to "free and fair" elections are not new. According to Bjornlund, for example, in 1927, the special emissary of US president "pledged the United States to a fair and free election" in Nicaragua, as part of an early effort at post conflict nation-building. In 1956, a United Nations report on a referendum on the future of Togoland, a trust territory in Africa, used the term. But the phrase apparently first achieved salience after the UN Security Council called for "the early independence of Namibia through free and fair elections under the supervision and control of the United Nations" in

1978 (Bjornlund). "Free and fair elections" has now become the catchphrase of journalists, politicians, UN officials, political scientists, etc.

Although the wave of democratisation in the early 1990's was accompanied by repeated insistence that elections should be 'free and fair', no clear and detailed definition of the constituent elements of a free and fair election was available though such a definition seems crucial. *"There is general agreement, among scholars and practitioners alike, that the essential feature, indeed the defining characteristics, of a democracy is free and fair elections. Where controversy arises is when we try to define these key terms in sufficient detail to provide a basis for assessing and -where necessary reforming- the actual operation of elections"* (Fletcher, 2007). The need for guidelines led the IPU (Inter-Parliamentary Union) to adopt, in 1994, the *Declaration on Criteria for Free and Fair Elections* which came to influence the development of electoral standards around the globe (Goodwin-Gill, 2006: v).

Since the 1990's, a number of other international organizations have attempted to better define "free and fair" elections or to articulate the standard's many components. For example, for the New Zealand Electoral Commission, 'free and fair' is the phrase commonly used when assessing elections in newly democratised countries"; (*Free and fair elections*, www.elections.org.nz). "Broadly speaking, 'free' means that there is no restriction on access to the process, and 'fair', that it is run impartially and in accordance with international standards." For the international organisation of Latin America, *Fronteras Comunes* (Common Borders),

•A *free* electoral process is one where fundamental human rights and freedoms are respected, including freedom of association, of assembly, freedom of speech and expression by electors, parties, candidates and the media, and also "freedom to and by electors to transmit and receive political and electoral information messages," etc.

A *fair* electoral process is one where the "playing field" is reasonably level and accessible to all electors, parties and candidates, and includes amongst others: an independent, non-partisan electoral organisation to administer the process, open and transparent ballot-counting, equitable and balanced reporting *by the media*, etc. ("What constitutes a Free and Fair Election?," Fronteras Comunes).

The 1990 Copenhagen document of the OSCE (Organisation for Security and Cooperation in Europe) set forth standards for free and fair elections in the 55 member countries. These require member countries to hold free elections at reasonable intervals, guarantee universal suffrage, ensure secret ballot for voting ensure that law and public policy permit a free campaign environment provide for *unimpeded access to the media*, amongst other things (Bjornlund).

Is the importance of media in/for Free and Fair Elections universally recognised?
It is a generally accepted fact that the media play a vital role during an election in a democratic context. Different provisions concerning the media are included in the IPU's *Declaration on Criteria for Free and Fair Elections* (Goodwin-Gill, 2006: vii - xi), amongst which:

• Article 3.4: Every candidate for election and every political party shall have an equal opportunity of access to the media, particularly the mass communications media, in order to put forward their political views
• Article 4.2: States should (...) encourage parties, candidates and the media to accept and adopt a Code of Conduct to govern the election campaign and the polling period
• Article 4.3: States shall ensure that
• "parties and candidates are free to communicate their views to the electorate, and (...) enjoy equality of access to State and public-service media.
• "That the necessary steps are taken to guarantee non-partisan coverage in State and public-service media"

According to the *Media and Elections Handbook* of the Institute for

Media, Policy and Civil Society (IMPACS) which is intended for reporters in northern as well as southern societies, "No Free Press = No Democracy" (2004: 6). A recent Report of the Media Council of Tanzania (*The Role of the Media in Reporting Elections*, August 2010), sums up the special relationship between democracy and a free media: "*They need each other. A free media will help keep the election honest and democratic. And a democratically elected government will protect the media's freedoms.*"

If in many regions today, a democratic election with no media freedom would be a contradiction in terms, in Africa, however, the media have not until recently been acknowledged as an important factor in the democratic process. "Discussions of democratization in Africa have often focused primarily on the formal state institutions: the public service, the judiciary, and the legislature. Scholars and activists have also shown concern on the role of civil society (…) However, little concern had been shown in the past on the media" (*The Role of the Media in Reporting Elections*, Media Council of Tanzania, August 2010).

The *African Charter on Democracy, Elections and Governance*, adopted in 2007, comprising 53 articles and 20 pages, contains only one line regarding the media: "*Promoting freedom of expression, in particular freedom of the press and fostering a professional media*" (p.11, article 27). It is the eighth of the ten commitments for State Parties to "advance political, economic and social governance." True, the Windhoek +20 campaign compliments efforts of a growing movement in Africa seeking, lobbying and influencing the adoption of Access to Information laws across the continent. But there still seems a long way to go.

The Human Rights' Perspective

From the Human Right's Perspective of the media and free & fair elections, three interlocking sets of rights, which are essentially all aspects of the right to freedom of expression guaranteed in Article 19 of the Universal Declaration of Human Rights, can be identified:

•the right of the voters to make a fully informed choice

•the right of the candidates/parties to put their policies across

•the right of the media to report and express their views on matters of public interest

It is to be noted that these apply at all times and not only around an election (Pratibha.com).

If it is today a truism to say that the media has an indispensable role to play in a democracy, it is still useful to examine its different aspects. Borrowing from various documents, we have tried to summarise some main media roles at election time in the table below.

Some main media roles during the elections

Role	How to fulfil these roles
Civic & Voters' Information/ Education	• Providing information on political knowledge, on political participation, and political learning in order that voters can make informed choices on how to use their votes • Information about the electoral system and process: how to exercise democratic rights and responsibilities, who and where to register, who can vote, how to vote, contest for office, etc. • How to make leaders accountable to their electoral promises and give the people the skills to audit how the resources of the country are used and by whom • Hold both the government and the opposition parties to account for how they have acted in the previous term. The people need to know how well the government has run the country since the last election, and what alternatives the opposition parties presented during that time

Enable full public participation in elections	• Analyse/scrutinize government actions/performance on past electoral promises and manifestoes, and holding them to account • Exposing irregularities through unfettered scrutiny of candidates/parties • Informing, educating and involving audiences
Direct access (candidates, parties to	• Providing a platform for political parties/candidates to communicate their platforms and views, policies and opinions to the electorate, and vice versa • Provide an arena in which candidates/parties can debate with each other

	through paid advertising) • Provide a right of reply to statements or reports in the media which were inaccurate or offensive • Political parties/ candidates should have equal opportunity, and no discrimination exercised against them
Provide voice/ feedback mechanism	• To provide a forum to debate with the public (citizens, NGOs, trade unions, experts), vox pop, interviews, etc.

An election watchdog	• Monitor the electoral process to report on the development of the election campaign • Report on the conduct of elections (how the elections have gone on) • Provide information/monitoring on vote counting • Report results • Report problems, investigate irregularities, expose foul play, corruption, election rigging, watch for Voters' rights, candidates' and party rights, and the election process, etc.
Plurality	• Offer plurality of views

2) Conditions for media to fulfil their roles around election time

Certain conditions are required for the media to be able to fulfil their roles, especially to function freely, fairly and independently. Berger, in a

discussion document compiled for SANEF (South African National Editors Forum) in 2002, identified the presence of six factors as necessary for the media as an industry and social institution to fulfil its role:

1. A legal dispensation that enables media freedom, some key dimensions of which are: freedom from censorship, freedom from arbitrary attack or interference, free access to meetings and a right to public information held by the State.

2. Media freedom or freedom of expression must exist in practice, complementing a free legal regime.

3. Independent media regulation that is free from government interference, and where publicly-funded media have an obligation to convey viewpoints of political opponents of the government.

4. General pluralism of media voices. This is generally interpreted as meaning that the media should be owned by a variety of interests

and that there should be equality of access to a wide range of media content amongst other things. The underlying principle is that the public need to be exposed to the widest variety of sources of information during an election in order for electoral choices to be real.

5.   Active journalistic professional bodies. The role of the professional bodies within the journalistic profession is important. These bodies can include journalists' or broadcasters' association, journalists' or broadcasters' trade unions, voluntary media councils, training institutions, amongst others. And, these bodies can develop codes of conduct specific to election matters.

6.   An audience that enjoys access to the media and freedom of expression, as well as has some respect towards the democratic role of media.

According to Berger, some of these elements are more relevant to the "free" dimension, others pertain to what constitutes "fair." All the conditions do not have to be perfectly met for an election to be free and fair, but it is difficult to imagine a "free and fair election" which fails to "fundamentally meet these media conditions." It is important to monitor the extent to which the six components, taken as a whole, impact upon the democratic event of an election. On the other hand, these six factors (or media components), even if they are all fulfilled, are not sufficient for an election to be free; they have to exist along with other aspects/conditions regarding funding of political parties, bribery or violence against voters, etc.

Egalitarian or Libertarian regime

The conditions for media to fulfil their roles will differ to a certain extent, depending upon the kind of regime: whether it is an egalitarian or a libertarian electoral regime - a distinction made in a landmark constitutional decision by the Supreme Court of Canada in 2004 (Fletcher, 2007).

The egalitarian regimes stress, as their primary value, *fairness*, i.e. they stress measures that promote the equality of the various participants in election campaigns, measured particularly in terms of their capacity to participate in electoral debate. The libertarian regimes stress as their primary value *freedom*, i.e. the freedom of the participants to use their own resources to influence the contest for power and influence. In practice, all electoral campaign regimes have elements of both models, but, according to Fletcher, countries like Canada, the UK and New Zealand tilt towards the egalitarian side, and the US and Australia to the libertarian side.

3) Free & fair elections: assessing media performance

The third part of this paper attempts to make a case for media monitoring/the assessment of media coverage of elections, to be carried out not just by international Election Observation Missions. Researchers, academics, national or other media analysts, etc. as well should be encouraged to carry out media monitoring and analysis of elections since this can provide a better watch on democracy which is a continuous process. It is to be noted, however, that Media Monitoring is only one way of improving media coverage in a democracy. There are other ways such as specific training for journalists to report elections.

There should be "monitors of the media, to ensure that the media meets its important responsibilities and that the election is free and fair" (Howard, 2004: 25). Monitoring of the media helps voters to know if they are well- informed by the media, allows the election commission and political parties to know that the media provides equitable and fair reporting for all parties, enables the international observers to know if reporting is without interference by the government or other powerful interests. Given that the media increasingly determine the political agenda, even in less technologically developed corners of the world, monitoring the media during election periods is becoming an increasingly common practice.

"Media monitoring must be done by respected and non-partisan or organizations with no personal gain or vested interest in who wins the election" (Howard, 2004: 25). As Bjornlund and others have suggested, observers should monitor all phases of the election process, including the pre-election period (including the informal or formal campaign period; the balloting and initial counting on Election Day); and the post-election phase (including the aggregation and tabulation of votes, the adjudication of complaints, and the formation of a new government). The approach and tools used by international Election Observation Missions can be much the same as those used for the international observer missions. The techniques used are often a combination of statistical analysis, techniques of media studies, and discourse analysis, to measure whether coverage has been free and fair.

The *Guidelines on Media Analysis during Election Observation Missions*, based on the observation activities of the Office for Democratic Institutions and Human Rights of the Organization for Security and Cooperation in Europe OSCE/ODIHR, and the Venice Commission (published by the Council of Europe & Venice Commission) describe in quite some detail a Media Monitoring Methodology. Borrowing largely from this document, we highlight below some aspects of the aims and objectives of Media Monitoring and a methodology.

Some general remarks concerning media monitoring:
- Media "monitoring" has to fit into the democratic process.
- Monitoring of media content is much more than simply monitoring the content of media coverage of an election campaign. There is a need to examine the specific political, economic, social and cultural contexts in which the media exist and in which free and fair elections are taking place.
- There is need to take into account the legal framework for the media, the national laws, the international standards adopted, etc.
- The media landscape must be taken into account.
- Media monitoring to ensure democracy has to take place around, during and *between* elections
- Whenever possible, the entire campaign period should be monitored. Or else, a careful choice should be made.

What Media Analysis of Election coverage tries to determine

Applying a variety of methods to gather the necessary information, the Media Analyst is concerned with, amongst others:

- the media conduct on the level of individual media organisations and journalists, but this has to be within the context of the media system as a whole
- how autonomous the media system is from the political system
- the level of diversity within the media system
- whether media coverage is balanced, fair, impartial, unbiased, etc.
- the media impact on the election.

When trying to determine these, the media analyst can ask a list of questions pertaining to:

- voters' right to receive information
- candidates' right to impart information
- the media's freedom of expression.

Voters' right to receive information

- Did voters receive sufficient accurate information from the media to make an informed choice?
- Did voters have the opportunity to consult a variety of sources of information with different points of view?
- Did the media provide voters with sufficient information on the election administration and voting procedures?
- Did the public/state media comply with their obligations to inform the public on relevant issues of the electoral process?
- Was there any preferential treatment for or against a particular candidate or party?
- Was there any prejudice in reporting based on ethnic, religious or gender issues?

The Candidates' right to impart information

- Were election contestants/parties given equal opportunity to

125

present their candidacies and platforms to the electorate through the media?
- Were they treated fairly by the media?
- Were programmes or coverage biased and if so, in whose favour?

The media's freedom of expression
- Did the media face any kind of censorship or obstruction by the authorities?
- Were journalists forced to adjust their comments or criticisms from authorities/editors/owners of media?
- Were any journalist or media harassed?

Although, ideally, it would be desirable to answer all the questions listed in the guidelines, however it is not always possible/feasible to answer all these questions.

The *Guidelines on Media Analysis during Election Observation Missions* recommend as methodology mainly interviews, quantitative and qualitative analysis

Interviews with journalists and other media professionals to collect, amongst other things:
- opinions on the regulations
- opinions on media coverage during the elections
- internal codes of conduct
- complaints received from parties or candidates

Quantitative Analysis
A number of quantifiable elements of media output can be collected, for instance:
- the amount of time devoted to particular politicians
- the length of time of parties' election broadcasts
- the number of times a particular word was used to describe a particular politician
- the number of women candidates quoted

- the number of times a particular campaign issue was reported

According to the *Guidelines*, other aspects of the media campaign coverage can also be usefully measured:
- number of mentions received by each political actor/candidate
- length of time or amount of space given to each actor/candidate
- positive, negative or neutral references to each actor
- references to different topics
- order of placement of news items on different candidates, parties, topics
- gender balance of media coverage of candidates.

Qualitative analysis of media coverage of the electoral process

The qualitative analysis can involve different topics:
- The coverage of opinion polls
- Voter education
- Episodes of hate speech and inflammatory language
- Journalistic style
- Professional conduct of journalists
- News omissions
- Analysis of formats used to cover the elections
- The advantage of the incumbent government

Examples of elements or questions that can be covered by the qualitative analysis are:
- Does a media outlet more or less openly support a party/candidate/referendum position? Which one?
- The weekly agenda of the media outlet: the most covered issues and how they are covered
- Any critical or analytical approach in providing political information, or do the media tend to report such information without any in-depth analysis?

• Episodes of defamation or hate speech

An overview of certain components of the *Guidelines on Media Analysis during Election Observation Missions* of the Venice Commission has been provided in the third part of the present paper. The full document provides much more detailed information. Other organisations as well have developed questions and tools pertaining to media monitoring at the time of election. We would like to quote some of the findings of the reports following a media monitoring exercise, in 2000 (*Elections 2000 Media Monitoring Project...*) and 2005 *The 2005 Elections in Tanzania*

Tanzania. The Media Monitoring Project in Tanzania was a joint undertaking by the Media Council of Tanzania, the Media Institute of Southern Africa-Tanzania Chapter, the Tanzania Media Women Association and the United Nations Association). To monitor and measure media output, standards were set out at three levels: international standards, the national law (Tanzanian law) and Code of Conduct.

The reports of the 2000 and 2005 Media Monitoring Project on Tanzania Elections show major areas in which the media had failed to live up to its tasks during election time. The reports point out that the media had failed:

• to provide relevant information to the electorate for them to make informed choices,
• were unable to provide the requisite space for people to express their opinions and views as stipulated in the code of conduct for elections reporting.
• voices of the people, the reports say, were almost never heard.
• the reports further point out that voters and civic education was inadequate.

The reports also pointed out that:
• the media remained mere amplifiers of what the politicians said, with little analysis or crystallisation of issues and platforms in

which the parties were fighting the elections on.

- there were cases of news blackout and suppression of stories negative to the ruling party especially in the state-owned and partisan media.
- little or no attention to women candidates or to issues affecting women were noted.
- overblown, sensationalized and misrepresented headlines, as well as instances of xenophobia and racism, were also noted in the media.

Several recommendations were made in the report, amongst others:

- Develop programmes to upgrade the skills and professional standards of journalists well in advance of the next elections.
- Training on elections reporting (for a more objective, truthful and conduct may assist the media to be more professional and ethical in its conduct.
- Media houses should institute ethical audits within newsrooms as part of the daily post-mortems to ensure compliance to the Code of Ethics for Elections Reporting
- Publicly-funded media must be detached from the control of the government of the day.
- The Tanzanian Broadcasting Corporation should develop clearer standards on the responsibilities of private broadcasters in covering election issues.

The Media Monitoring experience in Tanzania offers an enlightening example of the case we are trying to make concerning local media monitoring. Although the Tanzanian media system is far from perfect, it seems that we, in Mauritius, could learn a lot from this experience.

Bibliography/Reference:

African Charter on Democracy, Elections and Governance, http://www.un.org/democracyfund/Docs/AfricanCharterDemo crac y.pdf, accessed on 13 September 2010

Berger Guy., 2002, Media preconditions for free and fair elections, Discussion document compiled for SANEF, http://aceproject.org/ero-en/topics/media-and-elections/GuyBergerELECTION.pdf (accessed on 8 Sept 2010)

Bjornlund Eric, "Free and Fair Elections," Democracy International, http://www.democracyinternational.com/; (accessed on 2 Sept 2010)

Elklit, Jorgen & Svensson Palle, "What makes elections Free and Fair?" in *Journal of Democracy*, Vol 8, no 3, July 1997

Elections 2000 Media Monitoring Project, Interim Report, Media Council of Tanzania http://aceproject.org/main/samples/me/mex23.pdf, accessed on 5 September 2010

Fletcher Fred, "Free and Fair Elections: regulations that ensure a "fair go"," a talk given at the Parliament of Victoria, Melbourne, June 2007, www.sisr.net/publications/0706fletcher.pdf, accessed on 8 Sept 2010

"Free and Fair Elections," New Zealand electoral commission, http://www.elections.org.nz/elections/concepts/free-fair-elections/free-fair-elections.html, 30 August 2010

Goodwin-Gill Guy S., Free and Fair elections, New expanded edition, Inter-Parliamentary Union, 2006, http://www.ipu.org/pdf/publications/free&fair06-e.pdf, accessed November 2010

Guidelines on Media Analysis during elections observation missions, Europe Commission for Democracy through law (Venice Commission), http://www.venice.coe.int/docs/2005/CDL- AD(2005)032-e.asp, accessed on 10 September 2010

Guidelines on Media Analysis during elections observation missions, Europe Commission for Democracy through law (Venice Commission), http://www.venice.coe.int/docs/2009/CDL- AD(2009)031-

e.asp, accessed on 10 September 2010

Howard Ross (edited by Amanda Gibbs), 2004, *Media and Elections, An Elections Reporting Handbook*, IMPACS (Institute for Media, Policy and Civil Society), Vancouver, Canada, http://portal.unesco.org/ci/en/files18541/1130430234media_el ectio ns_en.pdf

Media & Elections, The Teaching Educators about Media (TEAM Project), http://www.edb.utexas.edu/resources/team/lesson_3.html, accessed 8 September 2010

Pinto-Duschinsky Michael, "Mass Media and Elections," http://www.democracy.ru/english/library/international/eng-1999-5.html, accessed on 8 September 2010

Report on Media Monitoring during election observation missions, European commission for democracy through law (Venice Commission), http://www.venice.coe.int/docs/2004/CDL-   AD(2004)047-e.asp, accessed on 10 September 2010

"Role of Mass Media During Election Time," by education consultants of pratibhaplus.com http://pratibhaplus.com/Articles.aspx?ArticlesID=191, accessed on 5 September 2010

The 2005 Elections in Tanzania mainland, http://www.tz.undp.org/ESP/docs/Observer_Reports/2005/T EMCO Report_Mainland_2005.pdf, accessed 8 September 2010

The Role of the Media in Reporting Elections, a report prepared for the Media Council of Tanzania, August 2010

"What constitutes a Free and Fair Election?," FronterasComunes (CommonBorders) http://www.commonborders.org/free_and_fair.htm, accessed on 28 August 2010

Windhoek+20, African platform on access to information, http://windhoekplus20.org..., accessed on 13 September 2010

18

New Spaces, New Challenges: The Relevance of Regulation

Krishna Oolun
Director of ICTA

The following text was transcribed from an audio recording of the speaker.

My paper will address the challenges of the new space of information and communication technologies and why regulation is fundamental in this area.

To begin with, the root of new space is the concept of disruptive technologies which break new frontiers with new concepts leapfrogging the way we do business in general.

It is here useful to state two laws of technology: the Moore's Law[39] and the Gilder's Law[40]. Those combined laws provide for information and telecommunication power which doubles every year, thus creating the new space we are referring to.

The formerly distinct entities which are classical telecommunications, broadcasting, the Internet and entertainment are now operating on a common platform thanks to convergence.

On top of that, demand from users is putting pressure on this new environment. Today, we can have anything over the Internet Protocol: voice over IP, image over IP, etc.

---

[39] **Moore's Law** states that the processing power of a microchip doubles every 18 months. It was formulated by Gordon Moore of Intel in the early 70's.

[40] **Gilder's Law** states that the total bandwidth of communication systems triples every twelve months. It was formulated by George Gilder, writer and co-founder of Discovery Institute.

Around two billion people in the world are already connected to the Internet and some 4.5 billion are connected to mobile phones in the world. These tremendous changes have brought about changes even in the way we entertain ourselves – we just have to look at the growing popularity of social networks (there are more than a hundred of them even for professional networks).

In this context, there are obviously some threats - the most important one being the fact that we cannot authenticate persons. Thus identity management is becoming a real issue.

We believe that a good regulatory framework is necessary in order to ensure secure communications for all through a series of technical regulations. For instance, the ICTA is currently working on a child protection platform and is following up the work done by the ITU (International Telecommunications Union) Council of Working Group on Child Protection. We are also looking at the public infrastructure to protect users when they are online. Other technical regulations are also important to curtail illegal and harmful content.

We are advocating a multi-stakeholder approach: we need to have the policy maker, an instance to seek redress if people are unhappy with a decision of the regulator, collaboration with operators and we do favour industry forum.

With the momentum gathered by this new space, we believe there is also a need for more consumer participation in all regulatory practice.

We need to note that in some countries, there are some drastic decisions taken with respect to Internet regulation, in a word, censorship. Fortunately, in Mauritius, there is no censorship at all.

In conclusion, this gives us food for thought for future directions and initiatives to better address issues related to this new space created by the Internet.

19

Les nouveaux habits (virtuels) du journaliste

Rabin Bhujun,
Rédacteur en chef de l'express dimanche

Le journal à papa est mort. Ou presque. Les lecteurs, surtout les plus jeunes, sont nombreux à le penser. Le journal papier traditionnel est « *has been* .» Parce que l'instantanéité est désormais la norme en matière d'information. On n'attend plus la sortie du journal, le flash info radio ou le journal télévisé pour se tenir informé. Le *news* est accessible en permanence à travers une multitude de supports. De l'iPad à Facebook et Twitter en passant par le téléphone portable ou les portails d'information sur Internet.

Cette révolution de l'information est en marche à l'étranger. Et occasionne depuis quelques années des dégâts irréversibles[41] aux journaux et à l'économie de la presse. Fermetures, réduction des effectifs de journalistes[42] et abandon du format papier[43] sont quelques-unes des conséquences de la nouvelle manière dont l'information – produit comme un autre – est désormais vendue et consommée.

L'industrie locale de la presse n'est pas encore entrée dans la phase critique où l'existence même des journaux papier est menacée. Mais la tendance se dessine. Parallèlement à la lecture des journaux, les Mauriciens ont davantage recours aux nouveaux médias[44] pour

---

[41] http://news.bbc.co.uk/2/hi/americas/7913400.stm
[42] http://www.telegraph.co.uk/finance/newsbysector/mediatechnologyandteleccoms/7557132/The-Guardian-newspaper-to-outsource-up-to-55-staff-to-cut-costs.html
[43] http://seattletimes.nwsource.com/html/businesstechnology/2008823971_onlinepapers07.html
[44] Conclusions du dernier sondage Media Focus (septembre/octobre 2010) réalisé par OpinionWay Maurice

s'informer. Conscients du fait que cette tendance va s'accentuer, les plus importants groupes de presse ont entrepris de ne plus se reposer seulement sur leurs produits papier et/ou radio. Ils se sont diversifiés en proposant une réelle offre d'information sur Internet. Est-ce à dire qu'à Maurice également le début de la fin des journaux papier a commencé? Certainement pas. Néanmoins, c'est sans doute la fin d'une certaine manière de concevoir et de pratiquer le journalisme.

Deux oasis dans un désert

Depuis 2008, le groupe La Sentinelle[45]et Le Défi Media Group[46]ont lancé leurs portails d'information. Alors que d'autres journaux[47]du pays se contentent de reproduire leur contenu papier sur leurs sites web, www.lexpress.mu et www.defimedia.info proposent non seulement les articles de leurs titres respectifs ; mais aussi du contenu spécialement écrit pour Internet. Des clips vidéo et audio sont aussi ajoutés en complément des textes. Ce qui permet à chacun des sites d'offrir une information multimédia à son audience.

Toutefois, si le groupe Défi Media s'appuie sur les journalistes de ses différents titres papier pour produire du contenu éditorial spécifique à son portail, le groupe La Sentinelle a adopté un modèle différent. En effet, le contenu *news* du site *lexpress.mu* est produit par une équipe dédiée de journalistes web. Ceux-ci couvrent au jour le jour l'actualité économique, politique et sociale. Et arrivent donc à proposer des informations et des mises à jour plus fréquentes que le site concurrent.

Si les approches commerciales[48] de leurs portails sont différentes, les journalistes des deux groupes fonctionnent de la même manière dans leur nouveau rôle de journalistes web ou journalistes en ligne. Ils

---

[45] Propriétaire et imprimeur de *l'express, l'express dimanche, 5 Plus dimanche, Essentielle, La Case…*
[46] Propriétaire et imprimeur de *Le Défi Plus, Le Défi Quotidien* et *L'Hebdo*
[47] Notamment *Le Matinal, Le Mauricien, Week-End, Mauritius Times*
[48] Seul le contenu web est gratuit sur *lexpress.mu*, la consultation des titres papier du groupe est payante. *Defimedia.info* opte pour le modèle gratuit complet mais n'offre en revanche qu'une sélection d'articles issue de ses titres papier à la lecture.

doivent satisfaire le besoin de base de l'internaute venu consulter leurs sites. Celui- ci est prioritairement à la recherche d'actualités chaudes. De « *hard news* ». Il veut avoir un accès immédiat à de l'information claire, directe, si possible avec des compléments son et image. Le journaliste web conscient de cela doit donc fournir un article informatif très rapidement après que les faits qu'il est chargé de rapporter se sont produits.

L'ère du web collaboratif permet de donner la parole aux internautes beaucoup plus facilement qu'aux lecteurs d'un journal imprimé. Ainsi, *lexpress.mu* et *defimedia.info* appellent tous deux leurs lecteurs à commenter les articles et éditoriaux mis en ligne. Chaque semaine, ces deux portails recueillent en conséquence des centaines de commentaires.

Mais proposer de l'information en permanence et permettre aux lecteurs de réagir rapidement à cette information revient-il à s'assurer de la survie du métier de journaliste ? Pas sûr. Si le journaliste papier est menacé d'extinction, le journaliste web fait lui aussi face à une nouvelle forme de concurrence. Celle de ses propres lecteurs !

Nous sommes tous journalistes!

L'affirmation sonne comme un défi aux journalistes professionnels. Le journaliste citoyen (*citizen journalist*) clame qu'il peut également rapporter, commenter et analyser l'information. Ceci grâce à l'apport de la technologie et des plateformes (Twitter, Facebook, blogs) qui lui permettent de toucher, en théorie, plusieurs millions d'internautes à travers le monde et des milliers ici, à Maurice. Cette affirmation tient-elle la route ? En partie, seulement.

Prenons quelques exemples. Une jeune étudiante de l'université de Maurice rentre chez elle dans un bus. Celui-ci est bloqué dans un embouteillage causé par un accident qui vient de se produire. Elle « twitte » en exclusivité l'information, car celle-ci n'est pas encore parvenue aux journaux et aux radios. Elle « twitte » une deuxième fois pour conseiller à ceux qui la lisent de ne pas emprunter ce tronçon de route. Indéniablement, elle a agi en « journaliste » en transmettant un message ayant une réelle valeur informative et pouvant être utile à d'autres citoyens.

Ce même type d'information peut-être relayé par Facebook ou à travers le blog d'une autre personne. En utilisant ces plateformes, les journalistes citoyens peuvent donc battre les journalistes web sur leur propre terrain, c'est-à-dire celui de l'information instantanée. La menace peut donc apparaître comme étant réelle. Mais en fait, elle ne l'est pas. Du moins pas dans l'immédiat.

De nombreux experts en journalisme ont affirmé[49] que le journaliste citoyen ne peut en effet s'assimiler au journaliste professionnel. Il peut tout au plus rapporter des « *breaking news* » dont il est témoin. Mais il est bien incapable de faire des analyses approfondies ou du journalisme d'investigation.[50] Une analyse sommaire de la blogosphère locale permet d'arriver à la même conclusion. Il y a deux explications à cela.

Premièrement une raison structurelle. L'accès à l'information (surtout auprès des administrations publiques) est très difficile. Les journalistes professionnels doivent régulièrement écrire des lettres officielles et obtenir des autorisations préalables auprès de hauts fonctionnaires avant que leurs interlocuteurs ne daignent répondre à leurs questions. Sans la sanction officielle d'un journal, il est peu probable que des journalistes citoyens locaux puissent, par exemple, avoir accès à des personnes ou des documents qui pourraient leur permettre de boucler une enquête sensible sur un service de l'État.

La deuxième raison est individuelle. Même sans être issus d'une école, les journalistes de métier apprennent les rudiments de leur profession sur le tas. Et se perfectionnent tout au long de leur carrière. Soit à travers la pratique ou lors de formations en journalisme. Ainsi, ils apprennent la nécessité de respecter une déontologie dans la manière de traiter et de présenter une information. De même, les journalistes chargés d'écrire des commentaires, des analyses ou des opinions sur des sujets d'actualité suivent tous un minimum de formation formelle (à l'université/en

---

[49] Interview with Richard Roher http://www.ourblook.com/Citizen-Journalism/Richard-Roher-on-Citizen-Journalism.html
[50] Interview with Professor David Weaver http://www.ourblook.com/Future-of-Journalism/David-Weaver-on-Future-of-Journalism.html

école de journalisme) ou informelle (en milieu professionnel) avant d'écrire ce type d'articles.

Ils s'approprient ainsi, par exemple, le principe voulant qu'une information soit vérifiée et contre-vérifiée avant de la transmettre aux lecteurs. Les journalistes formés comprennent également la nécessité de s'appuyer sur une documentation exhaustive ou une connaissance approfondie d'un dossier, bâtie au fil des années, pour émettre des commentaires, analyses ou opinions éclairés sur un fait d'actualité.

Il serait donc irréaliste de croire que le journaliste citoyen et le journaliste professionnel pratiquent la même discipline. Reprenons l'exemple cité plus haut de la jeune fille du bus. En apprenant qu'il y a eu l'accident, elle descend du bus. Et marche jusqu'aux véhicules accidentés. Elle fait des photos, notamment du chauffeur d'une des deux voitures impliquées dans l'accident. Elle le photographie, en gros plan, très grièvement blessé et coincé dans son véhicule. Elle croit comprendre, en écoutant la conversation des badauds amassés autour du lieu de l'accident, que le chauffeur de l'autre véhicule, sorti sans grandes blessures du carambolage, conduisait en état d'ébriété. Elle fait une photo de lui également.

Grâce à l'application web-publishing de son smart phone, la jeune fille écrit dans les minutes qui suivent un article pour son blog. Où elle explique le lieu, l'heure et les circonstances de l'accident tout en précisant que l'un des chauffeurs était ivre. Elle accompagne son texte des photos des voitures accidentées, du chauffeur grièvement blessé et de l'embouteillage que l'accident a créé.

Si pour le lecteur lambda tout ceci n'est finalement que du journalisme, cette manière de faire comporte une accumulation de manquements à la déontologie de la profession. Citons quelques exemples. Cette journaliste citoyenne rapporte sur son blog que le chauffeur d'un des véhicules était ivre. Face à un ouï-dire aussi grave, le journaliste professionnel serait dans l'obligation de vérifier l'information auprès d'une source autorisée : un policier ou un infirmier présent sur les lieux par exemple.

Ensuite, la journaliste a posté une photo d'une des victimes ensanglantée et coincée dans sa voiture sur son blog. Or, éthiquement, il est interdit aux journalistes de représenter une personne dans une position dégradante ou de faiblesse. Ce type de photo, choquante et dégradante, ne serait pas publiée dans un journal. Ce ne sont là que deux des manquements à la déontologie. Ils permettent toutefois de comprendre dans une certaine mesure en quoi l'approche du journaliste citoyen diffère de celle du journaliste professionnel.

Je blogue, tu blogues, nous bloguons…

Ce cas de figure reste toutefois théorique. Car dans leur écrasante majorité, les blogs locaux n'adoptent pas une approche journalistique. Ainsi, la plupart des blogs classés *(tableau 1 en fin d'article)* par le site Afrigator[51] se contentent de produire un contenu niche. *The Media Guru*[52] ou *Sjdvda*[53] reprennent (en commentant dans certains cas) les dernières nouvelles technologiques. Tandis que *Med Metal*[54] est entièrement consacré à la musique *heavy metal*. D'autres bloggeurs préfèrent l'approche « journal intime »[55] en racontant leur vie de tous les jours.

Les blogs les plus populaires du pays s'appuient sur l'optimisation de leur référencement (*search engine optimisation*[56]) pour accroître leur visibilité par les moteurs de recherche et donc leur trafic. Les sujets traités et les mots choisis dans leurs articles sont scrupuleusement étudiés afin d'augmenter le nombre de pages vues sur ces blogs. Ce qui peut leur permettre dans certains cas[57] de générer des revenus publicitaires.

Le contenu local et journalistique de ces sites est toutefois pauvre. Car leurs auteurs se contentent la plupart du temps de reprendre des informations déjà parues dans la presse sans les enrichir de faits nouveaux ou de commentaires élaborés. Occasionnellement, ils

---

[51] http://afrigator.biz/category/products/afrigator
[52] http://themediaguru.blogspot.com
[53] http://www.sjdvda.com/
[54] http://medmetal.blogspot.com/
[55] http://www.morinnbuzz.com/
[56] http://www.nouslesgeeks.fr/2010/11/08/le-seo-pour-les-nuls/
[57] http://www.islandcrisis.net

publient toutefois des sujets inédits. Qui s'apparentent à des coups de gueule[58] et sont plus proches du commentaire de l'homme de la rue que de l'analyse rigoureuse d'un commentateur aguerri.

La blogosphère locale abrite cependant bien quelques blogs animés avec un esprit journalistique. Leurs auteurs se donnent ainsi, par exemple, la mission de commenter l'actualité des médias et de la communication[59] dans le pays. Ou de décrire et décrypter des tranches de vie[60] locales. Ils font alors découvrir au lecteur du blog des faits et anecdotes insolites ou révélateurs de la culture et la manière de vivre dans le pays. Toutefois, non seulement ce type de blogs est rare mais bien souvent leurs auteurs abandonnent l'écriture sur leur blog, faute de temps. Ce qui mène irrémédiablement à une baisse de fréquentation de leur page web.

Dans l'ensemble donc, les blogs locaux ne semblent pas empiéter sur le territoire du journalisme. L'inverse n'est pas tout à fait vrai par contre. Depuis plus de deux ans, certains journalistes ont franchi le pas. En créant des blogs reprenant leurs articles publiés dans leurs journaux respectifs. Mais aussi en écrivant des articles, commentaires et analyses inédits spécifiques aux blogs. C'est dans cet esprit j'ai lancé mon blog[61] en septembre 2008. D'autres confrères[62] ont eu la même démarche.

Journaliste bloggeur, c'est quoi?

Une précision sémantique est nécessaire. On parle bien de journaliste bloggeur et non de bloggeur journaliste. Car les animateurs de ces blogs partagent d'abord leur travail journalistique tel qu'il est publié dans leur journal aux lecteurs sur le web. Parallèlement, ils utilisent les techniques journalistiques qu'ils ont acquises ainsi que des informations qu'ils peuvent avoir recueillies par ailleurs, pour traiter l'actualité ou l'analyser à travers des angles

---

[58] http://www.yashvinblogs.com/prisoners-conditions
[59] http://commaurice.wordpress.com
[60] http://mauricianismes.wordpress.com
[61] http://sansconcessions.wordpress.com/about
[62] http://www.doublethink.tk; http://enrasecampagne.wordpress.com

inédits.

Il est à ce sujet intéressant de noter qu'une polémique[63] a vite éclaté au sein de la blogosphère locale au sujet des journalistes bloggeurs. Des bloggeurs établis ont en effet eu tendance à dresser un cordon sanitaire autour des journalistes-bloggeurs. En arguant notamment que ces derniers ne pouvaient être considérés comme des bloggeurs. Et allant même jusqu'à prétendre que leur présence dénaturait l'esprit de la blogosphère locale. Depuis, la sérénité semble revenue parmi les bloggeurs.

Après plus de deux ans d'existence, je tire plusieurs leçons de mon activité de journaliste-bloggeur.

Premièrement, elle permet une interactivité accrue entre le journaliste et ses lecteurs. Les éditoriaux des différents titres de la Sentinelle sont accessibles dans la section « blog » de *lexpress.mu*. Les lecteurs y laissent des commentaires, par dizaines, chaque semaine. Or, le trafic dans cette section « blog » est particulier. Il est à sens unique ! En effet, seuls les lecteurs prennent la parole. Le format figé de cette section du site ne permet pas une interaction libre entre lecteurs et journalistes. Ces derniers n'interviennent d'ailleurs que dans de très rares[64] cas, notamment quand ils sont personnellement mis en cause dans certains commentaires.

Le blog est lui, tout au contraire, un espace de dialogue dans les deux sens. Alors que le ton des commentaires est plutôt déclaratif sur *lexpress.mu*, sur le blog, le lecteur devient interrogatif. Il questionne le journaliste sur ses choix. Sur ce qui l'a conduit à privilégier telle analyse plutôt que telle autre. Ce qui nous amène à la deuxième observation.

Deuxièmement, le blog devient un endroit où les choix éditoriaux et le fonctionnement du journal sont expliqués aux lecteurs. Ainsi, un article[65] consacré au Mauricien de l'année 2008 est vite devenu le prétexte pour expliquer le processus amenant mon journal à honorer une personne en particulier plutôt qu'une autre cette année-là.

---

[63] http://blog.metrolife7.com/2009/10/la-blogosphere-mauricienne-en- crise.html
[64] http://www.lexpress.mu/news/352-blog-ce-que-je-sais.html
[65] http://sansconcessions.wordpress.com/2008/12/28/cest-lhistoire-dune-couv/

Les journalistes réclament systématiquement de la transparence de la part des institutions. Or, ils ne s'appliquent pas nécessairement ce principe. Le blog du journaliste peut du coup devenir un excellent forum... pour rendre des comptes. Il m'est ainsi déjà arrivé de devoir m'expliquer[66] sur une erreur que j'ai commise dans un article au sujet d'un voyage du Premier ministre mauricien. A la lecture des commentaires, il apparaît clairement que les lecteurs ont pu comprendre comment et pourquoi l'erreur a été commise. Ce qui leur a d'ailleurs permis de mieux cerner le mode de fonctionnement et parfois les contraintes de la profession.

Troisièmement, le blog permet également au journaliste de montrer les facettes de son métier qui sont hors de portée du lecteur lambda et à propos desquelles celui-ci nourrit parfois des préjugés. La relation que les journalistes entretiennent avec les politiques est l'un de ces nombreux pans de notre métier que les lecteurs n'arrivent pas à cerner. J'ai pu ainsi écrire[67] sur le sujet afin d'amener ceux qui lisent le blog à réaliser que les postures publiques de défiance adoptées par les politiques n'ont parfois rien à voir avec la manière dont ils interagissent avec les gens de presse en coulisse.

De la même manière, certains changements dans un journal peuvent n'être rapportés aux lecteurs du format papier que dans une forme particulière ou sous un angle précis. Le blog permet lui de mettre en lumière d'autres aspects des coulisses d'un journal qui ne peuvent être tous publiés. Le changement de format[68] de *l'express dimanche* en février m'a ainsi donné l'occasion de raconter[69] en images, une partie du processus de fabrication du journal. Une phase de fabrication d'un journal que le grand public ignore.

Quatrièmement, le blog permet des modes alternatifs de «

---

[66] http://sansconcessions.wordpress.com/2009/09/27/la-photo-de-la-discorde/

[67] http://sansconcessions.wordpress.com/2008/09/30/%C2%AB-allo-je-vous-passe-le-ministre-%C2%BB/

[68] *l'express dimanche* est passé du format tabloïd imprimé sur du *newsprint* au format magazine tout en couleur à partir du 14 février 2010. D'autres changements sont à prévoir début 2011

[69] http://sansconcessions.wordpress.com/2010/02/14/les-coulisses du-nouveau-lexpress-dimanche/

storytelling ». En dehors des genres traditionnels de l'écriture journalistique que sont l'interview, le portrait et le reportage notamment. Le blog permet également de s'affranchir de la solennité qu'impose habituellement la fonction de rédacteur en chef. Dont les écrits engagent son journal. Le blog permet aussi bien d'écrire avec le « *gravitas* » de la fonction de rédacteur en chef que l'implication du citoyen lambda qui constate les dysfonctionnements d'une administration censée, par exemple, lui offrir un service de qualité.

Le blog permet donc d'utiliser la rigueur journalistique pour ensuite analyser certains faits dans une perspective individuelle. Ainsi, c'est en écrivant à la première personne que j'ai pu décrire comment les jeunes candidats[70] à une élection législative se comportent face aux journalistes pendant une campagne électorale.

Ce mode d'écriture à la première personne peut même prendre des accents de « journalisme de service ». Le journaliste, comme tout autre citoyen, doit parfois entreprendre des démarches administratives compliquées. Face auxquelles il se sent perdu. Du fait du nombre de documents à soumettre et des différentes administrations à contacter. J'ai ainsi profité de ma propre expérience avec l'administration pour partager[71] avec les lecteurs du blog les lenteurs administratives ou au contraire la célérité avec laquelle certaines d'entre elles fonctionnent.

Ces quatre particularités du fonctionnement du journaliste bloggeur aident donc à casser la dynamique haut/bas qui existe traditionnellement entre le lecteur (celui qui ne sait pas) et le journaliste (celui qui dit ce qu'il faut savoir). Au lieu de cela, une relation plus latérale est instaurée entre les deux parties. Une situation essentiellement au bénéfice du lecteur qui du coup, comprenant un peu mieux le fonctionnement du journaliste, se désinhibe et pose davantage de questions ou alors critique intelligemment le travail de son interlocuteur.

J'ai pu également constater que cette approche amène davantage

---

[70] http://sansconcessions.wordpress.com/2010/04/21/veux-tu-etre-mon-ami/
[71] http://sansconcessions.wordpress.com/2009/10/15/cwa-wma-ceb%E2%80%A6le-parcours-du-combattant/

144

d'internautes à s'intéresser aux blogs de journalistes. Un constat que partagent deux[72]33 de mes confrères. Dans mon cas, j'ai noté que de manière plus globale cette nouvelle plateforme d'interaction avec les lecteurs les conduit à revenir systématiquement vers le blog à chaque épisode d'actualité chaude.

Les statistiques de fréquentation (voir tableau 2 en fin d'article) de *sansconcessions.wordpress.com* démontrent ainsi que les lecteurs, informés par ailleurs par les sites des grands groupes de presse, affluent néanmoins vers les blogs dans des périodes riches en actualité. Ils voient dans les blogs de journalistes une source d'information complémentaire à défaut d'être alternative à celle des sites d'information locale. J'ai pu constater ce phénomène (cercle rouge de gauche dans le tableau 2) durant les jours précédents et suivant les élections législatives de mai 2010 à Maurice. Dans d'autres occasions (cercles du milieu et de gauche dans le tableau 2), la fréquentation du blog s'est considérablement accrue suite à des incidents[73]auxquels j'ai été personnellement mêlé ou à la suite de la publication d'un dossier[74]ayant suscité une vive polémique.

Quelles leçons tirer?

Il faut d'abord redire que le journaliste citoyen ne peut prétendre proposer un travail journalistique sans s'appliquer à avoir recours à quelques règles techniques et déontologiques. Pour le moment, toutefois, on ne peut pas dire qu'il y ait un mouvement vers la « journalisation » de la blogosphère locale. A ce titre le « journalisme citoyen » ne concurrence pas et ne menace pas de concurrencer la presse traditionnelle ou les sites d'information locale.

Toutefois, dans leur stratégie Internet, les entreprises de presse doivent prendre en considération et comprendre la demande des lecteurs et des internautes pour une plus grande interaction avec les

---

[72] C'est le cas des animateurs des blogs http://enrasecampagne.wordpress et www.doublethink.tk

[73] http://sansconcessions.wordpress.com/2010/06/13/imbecillites

[74] http://sansconcessions.wordpress.com/2010/09/06/le-vrai-pouvoir-des- castes-a-maurice/

journalistes qu'ils lisent ou écoutent. Pour l'heure, les sites web d'information locale ne ressentent pas la nécessité de formaliser, comme cela à été fait ailleurs, des modes de collaboration plus étroits[75] entre journalistes web et journalistes citoyens. Mais quelques pistes concrètes peuvent néanmoins être explorées.

1. Il s'agit d'abord de créer du trafic à deux sens autour des articles et éditoriaux publiés. Instaurer un dialogue entre le monde du journalisme (perçu comme étant fermé sur lui-même) et les lecteurs des sites web.

2. Il faut également permettre aux lecteurs de lancer eux-mêmes des sujets de discussion ou des thèmes de débat destinés à être repris sur les sites d'information. La création de forums interactifs sur les sites d'information pourrait contribuer à placer les préoccupations des lecteurs au centre du travail des journalistes.

3. On peut également penser créer des moments d'interaction directe entre journalistes/éditorialistes et les lecteurs des sites et des journaux. Notamment à travers l'organisation régulière de chats autour de thèmes précis d'actualité ou même de sessions « d'actualités commentées » en ligne, modérées en temps réelle par les journalistes.

4. Les sites d'information peuvent également penser à «semi-professionnaliser » les journalistes citoyens en leur offrant des plateformes de blog au sein même du site d'information. Par exemple sous la formule http://monblog.lexpress.mu.[77]Ceci peut avoir le double avantage pour les sites d'information de fidéliser et de se rapprocher des journalistes citoyens. Alors que ces derniers, opérant des lors sur une plateforme hébergée par des professionnels, seront amenés à adhérer à des standards minimum de déontologie et de règles journalistiques rudimentaires.

A peine né, le journaliste web mauricien n'est pas encore menacé de mort. Pour assurer sa longévité, il lui faut toutefois comprendre qu'il lui faut faire des journalistes citoyens ses partenaires. Avant que

---

[75] http://www.poynter.org/content/content_view.asp?id=83126
[76] Les journaux *Le Monde* ou *Le Figaro* proposent déjà ce genre de service
[77] Les journaux *Le Monde* ou *Le Figaro* proposent déjà ce genre de service

ceux-ci ne finissent par devenir ses concurrents…

Tableau 1

Top ranked blogs on Afrigator

1. Yashwin, pages of my life
2. The Media Guru
3. Island Crisis
4. Sans Concessions
5. Something to talk about.
6. En Rase Campagne
7. A Restless Mind
8. The Eagle's Lodge - Mauri
9. sjdkda's blog
10. Media et Communication à
11. 7PHP dot COM
12. Knight-Nirvan
13. – doublethink –
14. Nirvanknight™
15. Bruno's Mauritian Blog
16. Hello World
17. Your needs end now
18. Med Metal
19. The GMedia
20. iNcoRpoRate dRiFt

➡ View detailed Afrigator statistics

Tableau 2

Stats: Sans concessions

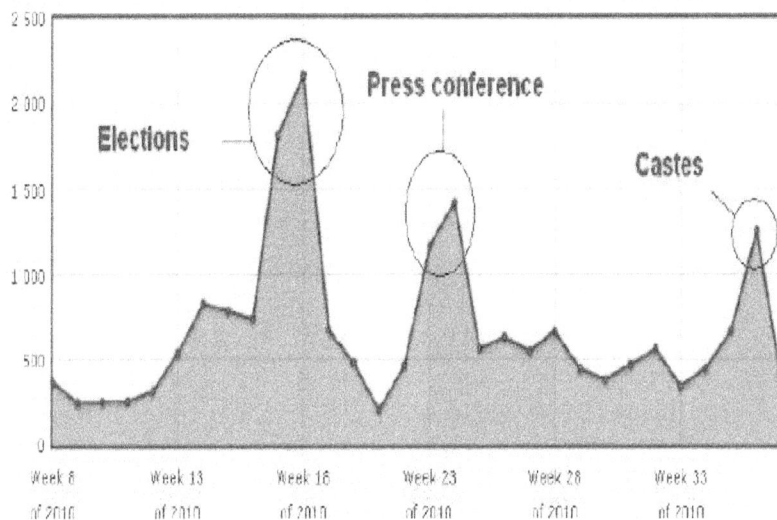

148

Citizen journalism as a means to make people think

Avinash Meetoo
Managing-Director of Knowledge Seven (www.knowledge7.com)

The Mauritian education system tends to create people who are passive. But, lately, it has become important to find ways to make people start thinking by themselves instead of always relying on others to make decisions for them.

As the economic and political events in the past few years have shown, it is impossible to predict how the world will evolve and countries which are not agile enough will definitely suffer. People in Mauritius need to innovate, create wealth and, thus, make the country change its course towards prosperity again. But to be innovative, one has to be able to think and express oneself freely.

One possibility is through citizen journalism. Having a website on an essential theme (e.g. economy, society, politics, etc.) while letting people contribute articles and engage in discussions with others freely is one way to help them become free thinkers.

During the past general elections in Mauritius, my wife and I set up such a website called *www.elections.mu* and the main theme was, of course, politics. During three weeks, 33 articles were written and each had 23 comments on average. Interestingly, only a negligible number of comments were rejected by the moderators. I noticed that the discussions were of high quality and not blindly partisan.

In our opinion, it is essential that people in Mauritius be given opportunities to think and express themselves freely. In the future, I would like to extend this experiment to other themes.

Citizen journalism

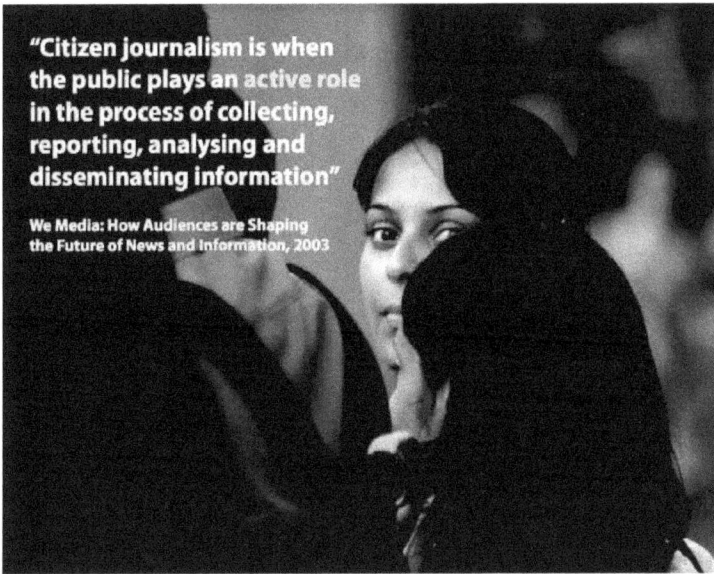

"Citizen journalism is when the public plays an active role in the process of collecting, reporting, analysing and disseminating information"

We Media: How Audiences are Shaping the Future of News and Information, 2003

As authors Bowman and Willis say[78]: "The intent of this participation is to provide independent, reliable, accurate, wide-ranging and relevant information that a democracy requires."

In the Mauritian context, citizen journalism is also a way to compensate for the problems that exist in our education system. It is not normal for someone who have gone though thirteen years of schooling (primary + secondary) to believe that "the others above" will always have solutions to his/her problems. People in Mauritius need to realise that the prosperity of a country depends above all on the amount of innovation taking place in it. And, for innovation to take place, people need to be free to think (out of the box).

Wikipedia is, by far, the largest and most successful citizen journalism project.[79] On Wikipedia, anyone can contribute articles and amend existing ones. Of course, it is possible that someone might contribute false information to Wikipedia but, if this happens,

---

[78] http://www.hypergene.net/wemedia/weblog.php?id=P36
[79] http://en.wikipedia.org/wiki/Special:Statistics

anyone can undo this action (or, most probably, correct it). Wikipedia now has more than 23 million pages which were edited nearly 450 million times by 14 million different users.

AgoraVox[80], created by Carlo Revelli and Joël de Rosnay in 2005, is a news website where anyone can submit articles on various topics. Moderation is done by authors who reckon at least four published articles.

www.elections.mu

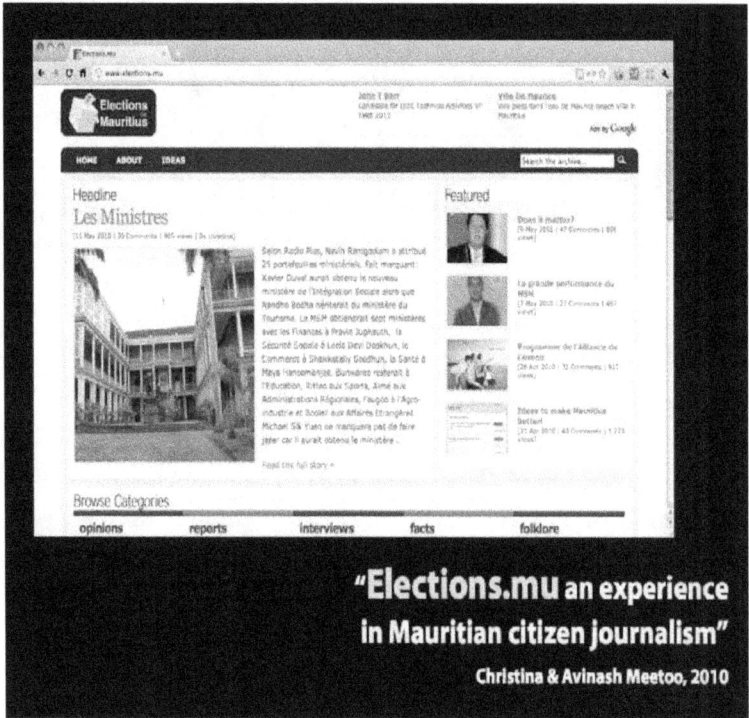

"Elections.mu an experience in Mauritian citizen journalism"
Christina & Avinash Meetoo, 2010

*www.elections.mu*4 was launched on 18 April and, less than three weeks later, had 33 articles written by five contributors. The total number of comments was 757, which means that an article had 23 comments on average. Interestingly, the comments were of very high

---

[80] http://www.agoravox.fr/

quality. Most of them were not overly partisan and only a few (less than 10) had to be rejected because of their tone or defamatory nature.

During the three weeks, *www.elections.mu* was viewed 20,947 times with a peak on 5 May 2010, the day the general elections took place in Mauritius. People spent 4 minutes on the website (which is a lot in our era of skimming...) and visited an average of 3 pages.

One essential aspect of *www.elections.mu* was that people could contribute "ideas to make Mauritius better"[81] This specific section now has more than 200 ideas submitted by more than 250 different people.

www.elections.mu became popular very quickly and got quite a lot of media coverage as it was featured in four different newspapers including in one on election day!

Self policing

"Self policing: monitor one's own adherence to legal and ethical standards, rather than have an outside agency to monitor and enforce those standards."

Wikipedia.org

---

[81] http://www.elections.mu/ideas/

I strongly believe in self policing as opposed to having laws to dictate what Mauritians can say online. There are many reasons for that, both technical and social. On a technical level, it should be noted that most websites regularly accessed by Mauritians (including *www.elections.mu* during the elections) are hosted outside Mauritius.

On a more social level, I believe people in Mauritius can engage in self policing because we are mature, we are responsible and we are intelligent as demonstrated by the fact that discussions were always of high quality on *www.elections.mu* even though the topic chosen (i.e. the general elections in Mauritius) created a lot of passion.

Why citizen journalism is essential

"Let's Make A Better World"
Michael Jackson, "Heal the World", 1991

My intention when I launched *www.elections.mu* (as well as my other websites[82] was to create a better Mauritius for the next generation. The strategy is to offer Mauritians a platform where they have freedom of thinking and freedom of speech. In this way, they

---

[82] http://www.knowledge7.com/, http://www.noulakaz.net/, http://www.infos.mu/, http://www.threebags.com/

can develop the mental aptitudes which will allow them to innovate and to bring progress, prosperity and additional stability to the country.

For me, citizen journalism is not a finality. It is only a means towards a better future for all of us.

21

The Emerging Digital Environment: Opportunities and Constraints

Azhagan Chenganna
Lecturer at the University of Mauritius

The surrounding ideologies about internet, social media and online interactions tend to indicate that the democratization of modes of production on the net is likely to provide opportunities for "citizen journalism" and that a "new participatory culture" is probably unfolding. Without challenging these promises, this paper focuses on the opportunities and constraints in the digital environment. It spells out the opportunities on the premise that citizens including journalists stand ready to engage and harness the power of the digital sphere. In a second part the paper elaborates on the structural constraints that hinder the development of a digital environment in Mauritius.

A number of recent events give credence to the idea that citizen journalism provides opportunities to better inform and mobilize the public. If Cottle (2009, XI) argues that it is difficult to define exactly what is meant by "citizenship" and "journalism," he states that citizen journalism is tied to the global civil society and "has evolved rapidly across recent years and is expressive of the surrounding culture, organizational structures, and politics of civil societies." A defining feature of citizen journalism is that it is based on connectedness characterized by low-cost, portable and digitized communication technologies that are easily plugged into and uploaded to the worldwide web. In addition, citizen journalism is combining with conventional journalism and global news flows as traditional media connect with the blogging masses and user generated contents of digitally active audiences. Despite reluctance of mainstream media "to surrender their traditional editorial control [...]," Cottle argues that generally news organizations "are cognizant of the added value that forms of citizen journalism can now bring when packaged inside their own news presentations."

Citizen journalism

In defining citizen journalism, Allan and Thorsen (2009, 7) note that there is a critical link between citizen journalism and crises. According to them, it is in situations of crises that "ordinary people are compelled to adopt the role of reporter" and as activists "their motivation is to bear witness to crisis events unfolding around them." The Iranian protests in 2009 can showcase their argument. Iran's disputed elections in June 2009 brought to the attention of the world the vibrant ways new media can be used to unleash the forces of ordinary citizens. Iran has some 700,000 bloggers and according to Sreberny and Khiabany (2010) social media such as Twitter, Facebook, and Youtube had played a crucial role in the green uprising to mobilize protesters against the Iranian regime. In addition, the graphic footage of the death a young Iranian woman by the name of Neda, captured by ordinary citizens with their cell phones, circulated widely on the blogosphere. Commenting on the fatal event, a CBS News reporter wrote : "The footage, less than a minute long, appears to capture the woman's death moments after she was shot at a protest - a powerful example of citizens' ability to document events inside Iran despite government restrictions on foreign media and Internet and phone lines" (CBS, 2009).

Wiki-activism has also the power to bolster investigative journalism. For instance, the whistleblower site *Wikileaks* allows sources across the world to publish secret documents that disclose injustice, abuse and corruption. Over the past four years since its existence, *Wikileaks* has been successful in the publication of a number of scoops. Amongst other things, it has released documents raising awareness about the shooting of innocent civilians by US military in what is now known as the Afghanistan War Logs Affairs. It has also uncovered the toxic waste dumped by Trafigura.

Can citizen journalism be a tool for social transformation? Some critics doubt that social networks such as Twitter are likely to stimulate real change. Digital skeptics argue that the social networks amplify the new, but fail to decipher the complexity of the world which requires gradual and sustained attention. They state that citizen journalists will never replace real news.

Then, what are the consequences for news cultures? If citizen journalism offers the possibility to better inform and mobilize the public, doubtless to say that the ethics of journalism is as important online as in the offline world. The challenge for journalists as well as citizens is how to authenticate sources on the internet in an era where information is available in real-time? How to ensure the credibility of sources when communication and public relations agencies are constantly trying to spin and control news events? How to process and vet information from Twitter, RSS Feeds, SMS and E-mails? These questions will have to be addressed if journalism is to remain trusted and to avoid lapses in quality.

In Mauritius, the digital space is still burgeoning. Critics say that the blogosphere is too polarized. However, it can be said without doubt that the new digital sphere can enrich conventional journalism by providing a diversity of sources and voices that remained unheard.

Regulatory Constraints

One of the major constraints facing the digital environments in developing countries is the kind of regulatory frameworks in which the telecommunications and the media sector operate. In fact, ineffective regulation can be an obstacle and stifle the growth in the digital sectors and can fail the goals of communication policy.

Hills (2005) notes that regulation in the sector should emphasize "independent regulation [...] which is participatory and not hostage to any political and economic interests." Regulation imposes rules to operate in markets. Historically, the process of liberalization of telecommunications was spearheaded in industrialized economies and was later exported to developing countries through the World Trade Organisation (WTO) Agreement of 1997. The latter has been a harbinger to the opening up of the telecommunications sector to private companies in many African countries.

In Mauritius, it is in the 2000's that the telecommunication sector was liberalized with the licensing of private players in the sector, besides the national telecommunications carrier. In the broadcasting sector, three private radio stations were allowed to operate while television is still under the control of the state. In the wake of the deregulation in the telecommunications and the partial liberalization in the broadcasting, two new regulatory agencies were set up, namely the *Information and Communication Technologies Authority* (ICTA) and the *Independent Broadcasting Authority* (IBA).

In fact, the national regulatory frameworks that have been established have not provided for more competition and better choice to citizen-consumers. For instance, the *Information Communication Technologies Authority* (ICTA) holds that it aims to "play a leading role in the future of ICT in Mauritius contributing to an efficient, competitive and optimally regulated ICT sector" (ICTA, 2010). Its mission as spelt out on its website is to promote ICT services through market-driven competition."

However, since the liberalization of the telecommunications sector in the 2000s, competition in the telecommunications and digital sectors have been hardly existent. The historic telecommunication operator – Mauritius Telecom – still remains the dominant operator with a significant market share. The entrance of a few new players in the telecommunications market may justifiably be considered to have constituted a cartel market in the national telecommunications and internet services sectors. If telecommunications policy and the regulation by the Information and Communication Technologies Authority (ICTA) could have stimulated market efficiency and greater investment in the sector, this has not yet been the case.

The independence of the regulatory authorities and transparent and credible regulatory mechanisms will have to be established to allow the development of efficient telecoms and internet services markets. In fact, since its creation, the ICTA has suffered from regulatory capture - it has maintained a status quo in the sector which is largely benefiting the dominant historic operator. Its regulatory approach has failed to be proactive. As a result, the telecommunications and internet services sectors in Mauritius are being held back by the historic operator and this stifles the opportunities in the sector for both private operators interested to invest in the market and citizen-consumers who expect to have a larger choice in internet services. Similarly, broadcasting regulation is being repressed by regulatory capture with the monopoly of the national broadcaster on television broadcasting. The existing regulatory environments restrain the opportunities of citizens to benefit from the potentials of the new digital era.

Access and Inclusion

The question of access to broadband services remains equally a major challenge for the development of digital environments. New forms of inequalities are being created with those who have access to broadband facilities and those who don't. A recent report from the Broadband Commission (2010) emphasizes the need for broadband inclusion. It states that "broadband inclusion for all will represent a momentous economic and social change [...] and that it will be a game changer in addressing rising healthcare costs, delivering digital education for all, and mitigating the effects of climate change [...]." It goes on to state that "broadband must be anchored around the concept of knowledge societies, including principles of freedom of expression, quality education for all, universal access to information and knowledge of and respect for cultural and linguistic diversity. Equitable and affordable universal access to broadband networks and broadband enabled applications are key for the delivery of online public goods and services, the sharing of scientific information, the strengthening of social cohesion and the promotion of cultural diversity."

In Mauritius, the intent of building knowledge societies has to be accompanied by coherent policy framework which provides greater access to broadband services to citizens. Cost, affordability of broadband, geographical availability, lack of skills, equipments can be

159

major barriers to digital inclusion. According to a Central Statistics Office report (2009) some 64% of households with no computer at home reported that a computer was not necessary, while 31% of households say that a computer is too expensive for not buying one. Around 72% of households with no computer did not have the intention to buy one. In 2008 among households with computers, 67.5% had access to Internet. The two most common mode of Internet access were dial up (48%) and ADSL (40.5%). Amongst households not having Internet connection some 79% reported that they did not intend to obtain Internet connection; 15.3% intended to have access after one year and 5.4% within the next twelve months (CSO, 2009).

Policy makers in the communications sector have to promote the emergence of digital cultures through better access to internet services and digital participation of all. Amongst other things, wifi zones would be beneficial. Digital media literacy has to be promoted. Projects such as the 'community cyber cafes' have to re-ignited and the government's policy of ensuring of *one lap top per child* should be implemented in order to enlarge the circle of digital opportunities to all.

Conclusion

This paper has highlighted some of the opportunities and constraints in the emerging digital environment. It has dwelt on the potentials of citizen journalism. While elaborating on some of the arguments of digital skeptics who state that citizen journalists will never replace real news, the paper has also highlighted the likely impact of citizen journalism on conventional journalism. Some of the constraints in the digital sphere have also been flagged. It has been argued that regulatory frameworks and approaches adopted by regulatory agencies can restrain digital opportunities and that instead, policy makers should promote digital access and inclusion of all to the benefit of society.

References

Allan, S and Thorsen, E (2009) *Citizen Journalism : Global Perspectives.* P. Lang Publishing, NY

Broadband Commission (2010*) A 2010 leadership Imperative: A future built on Broadband.* [online, www.broadbandcommission.org]. 12 oct 2010

CSO (2009) *Economic and Social Indicators. Information and Communication Technologies Statistics.* Mauritius

Cottle, S (2009) Series Editor's Preface. In Allan. S and Thorsen. E (Eds) *Citizen Journalism : Global Perspectives.* P.Lang Publishing, NY, IX-XII

Hills, J (2003) *Regulatory models for broadcasting in Africa.* UK

ICTA [online, www.icta.mu].12 oct 2010

Sreberny, A and Khiabany, G (2010) *Blogistan : The Internet and Politics in Iran.* I.B Tauris, London

22

Training and Professionalism

Kiran Ramsahaye
Editor-in-Chief of Le Matinal

The following text was transcribed from an audio recording of the speaker's presentation.

To understand the issue we are discussing today, we need to go back to the kind of revolution that has happened to the media industry in Mauritius over the past 7-8 years. Prior to that period, the media landscape was different; we had a very restricted landscape. This changed dramatically with the arrival of private radio stations and subsequently other print media. With these new players ushering in, naturally journalists were on demand.

Alas, we do not have a training institution that would provide the kind of training practising journalists would require. We have relied mostly on training on the job. There are by the way some schools of thought that journalists coming from training institutions from overseas are too academic. Very few in the profession have actually had formal training in journalism. In my institution, I do not have a single journalist who has been trained by an established institution in the media. But we do insist on a minimum requirement of a university degree if anything. One has to mention here the case of the current editor-in-chief of *L'express* who holds a Masters in Physics. Most of us do not have any formal training in journalism, like in other fields (such as architecture, medicine, etc.).

The challenge today is on a daily basis. Writing is only one aspect of the profession. It is a common misconception that having the aptitude to write makes you a journalist. I know people who find it difficult to put a sentence together but who are excellent news gatherers. After all, newspapers is a business of collecting and transmitting news.

We do complain that we do not have trained people but we do what we can by investing in new recruits in terms of resources, on the job training, and in house training. And when the opportunity comes across, we do send them overseas to follow crash courses.

I must here pay tribute to my colleague Jean-Claude de l'Estrac who as president of the Media Trust worked a lot to ensure that we had ongoing training for practising journalists. It is now unfortunate that the fate of the Media Trust does not allow this anymore.

We actually need to say our mea culpa in the profession. We are not perfect or infallible. I myself read my newspaper at 5 a.m. every morning and believe me it's an ordeal. The same applies to all other papers. The Chief Editors are never satisfied of the quality of the news. We are not satisfied that the journalists brought enough information and elements which would be of interest to readers.

But if we had formal training institutions, with people having both academic and practical training, this would have changed significantly the face of the industry.

Today, about less than 8-10% in the profession have any formal training in terms of full academic tertiary training in the field of journalism. I myself do not have such training as well as others. Yet we endeavour to do our best.

Journalists have an important task to ensure that the information being transmitted is correct. We have no business giving out incorrect info. I am not here referring to opinion and views. This is another matter. The most essential component of a newspaper is the news,. Are we sufficiently trained to ensure that rigour and full proof accuracy is there? This is where the real challenge lies.

23

Presse et Formation: Du journaliste au « journanalyste »

Jean-Claude de l'Estrac
Président du conseil d'administration de La Sentinelle Ltée

Une première évidence s'impose : du fait des nouvelles technologies de l'information, les journaux ne sont plus ce qu'ils étaient. Il en découle que les journalistes doivent se transformer, se transmuer. Ils ne font plus le même métier.

Il est couramment considéré qu'un journal, c'est essentiellement l'organisation de la collecte et la publication de « news ». Aujourd'hui, c'est faux si par « news ," nous entendons la primeur et la fraîcheur de l'information. Depuis toujours, les écoles de journalisme nous enseignent que les informations, les « news », ont cela de commun avec le poisson ou la salade, que plus elles sont fraîches, meilleures elles sont !

Or, il n'y a presque plus personne pour découvrir une information dans son journal. Cela arrive encore, mais ce sera de plus en plus rare. Dans le nouveau paysage médiatique, l'information est partout, instantanément disponible. Elle est accessible, souvent gratuite, abondante. Un sondage mondial réalisé par une association de presse a récemment indiqué la mesure de cette révolution: la majeure partie de la planète a pris connaissance de la mort de Michael Jackson non pas par des journaux, ni même la télévision, ni la radio, ni l'Internet, mais par... le téléphone portable ! Hier, l'information était une denrée à consommer une fois toutes les 24 heures. L'information, désormais, c'est ici et maintenant. Nous sommes dans l'ère de l'immédiateté. Personne n'attend un journal qui paraît une fois par jour pour connaître l'état du monde. L'information, c'est ce qui est transmis en temps réel.

Cette nouvelle donne force les journaux à se réinventer. C'est le journal britannique « The Guardian » qui a peut-être le mieux résumé ce nouvel enjeu. Il a expliqué que les « newspapers » sont morts, mais que vient le temps des « viewspapers » ! C'est là tout le paradoxe. Plus l'information est abondante, véhiculée par de très nombreux supports, plus elle est accessible, produite par qui veut – le soi-disant journalisme citoyen -, plus il faudra des professionnels pour l'authentifier, la valider, la décrypter, la hiérarchiser, lui donner du sens, la mettre en perspective, l'interpréter, l'analyser, l'éditorialiser. Il s'agit d'un travail de spécialiste. C'est ainsi que le journaliste devient un « journanalyste ».

Cette transformation du métier n'est pas facilement réalisable. Quand quelques débrouillards, collecteurs d'informations dotés d'un bon réseau de contacts, d'une maîtrise approximative de la langue et d'un peu de culture générale pouvaient prétendre exercer le métier de journalistes, il n'en est pas de même pour les « journanalystes » du temps nouveau. Il leur est demandé une grande acuité d'analyse, une parfaite maîtrise de l'expression, un sens de l'histoire et une vaste culture générale. Cela ne peut pas s'obtenir, sauf dans quelques cas exceptionnels, sans une longue formation. L'absence d'accès à cette nécessaire formation est la principale faiblesse de la presse mauricienne.

Ce manquement a toujours existé. L'absence de véritable école de formation, la rareté des stages de perfectionnement à l'étranger, la paralysie depuis quelques années du Media Trust, le seul organisme chargé de la formation des journalistes, ont pesé négativement sur la qualité de la presse mauricienne. Il est remarquable qu'en dépit de ces vrais handicaps, les journalistes mauriciens indépendants ont globalement produit une presse vivante, nerveuse, vigilante et responsable. On peut même arguer que la presse mauricienne a puissamment contribué au développement du pays tout au long de ses 237 années d'existence. A Maurice, la presse est aujourd'hui l'un des principaux forums du débat public, un foyer de cohésion sociale, un vecteur d'unité nationale. Sa pluralité et la vivacité des débats qu'elle anime font d'elle l'institution la plus démocratique du pays.

Les Mauriciens reconnaissent parfaitement cette contribution, ils sont plus de huit sur dix à considérer qu'elle joue un rôle positif dans le pays (Sondage Media Focus, mars 2010).

Mais pour assumer le rôle que lui imposent les nouvelles technologies de l'information, pour produire les « journanalystes » de demain, il faut régler d'urgence la question fondamentale de la formation. L'Université de Maurice devrait assumer cette responsabilité. Nous parlons ici de véritable formation, d'études de longue durée. Il faudrait recruter des étudiants de haut vol et les faire sponsoriser par des groupes de presse qui le peuvent. Il faudrait que l'Université de Maurice puisse conclure des accords de partenariat avec des écoles de journalisme d'autres pays. Et surtout qu'elle se rapproche de l'entreprise pour bien mesurer ses besoins et ses attentes. La transmission à la société du savoir universitaire est absolument indispensable, plus encore dans le cas qui nous préoccupe que dans d'autres. Là encore, les « journanalystes » joueraient leur rôle de «médiateurs ."

On ne mesure pas suffisamment à Maurice ce qui est exigé d'un futur journaliste. Dans les pays que nous connaissons le mieux, en Angleterre, en Inde, en France, on ne devient journaliste qu'au bout de longues études, suivies après avoir été reçu à des concours extrêmement sélectifs dans certains cas. Les écoles recrutent des étudiants du niveau HSC + 2, avant de les former pendant cinq, voire sept ans. A condition, bien sûr, qu'ils aient passé le concours d'entrée ; en France, pour certaines écoles, on compte jusqu'à un millier de candidats pour 50 à 60 admis. La formation assurée est très large. Un exemple, le programme de l'Asian College of Journalism de Delhi : trois ans de cours destinés à des licenciés – on y apprend « *the role of journalists in society, the ethical decisions they are called to make, the value of media diversity and pluralism* » ou encore « *important aspects of international relations...* » et de manière fort pertinente pour nous, « *the struggle between secularism and pluralism on one hand and communalism and religious fundamentalism on the other hand* ».

On voit l'ampleur de ce dont il s'agit, bien au-delà de l'apprentissage des techniques d'écriture journalistique. Pour un journaliste mauricien, les connaissances exigées sont aussi complexes.

167

Comment peut-on prétendre exercer le métier de « journanalyste » sans une connaissance approfondie de l'histoire politique et économique du pays? Dans un pays pluriethnique et multireligieux comme le nôtre, comment « analyser » quoi que ce soit sans des notions d'ethnologie et d'anthropologie? Sans avoir une connaissance des théories de l'ethnicité? Comment parler des « communautés » sans connaître les pays d'origine des Mauriciens, leur histoire, leurs pratiques et coutumes? Comment analyser et éclairer le débat public sans avoir approfondi soi-même les problématiques de l'ethnie, de la race et de la nation? De l'histoire des religions? Sans comprendre la sociologie des sociétés multiculturelles? Comment commenter sans appréhender les valeurs de la République? Le sens de l'État laïc? Comment situer la place et le rôle de Maurice sans chercher à comprendre les enjeux géostratégiques et la pratique des relations internationales? Comment hiérarchiser, relativiser, nuancer sans références universelles? Comment faire sans beaucoup lire, ni beaucoup voyager?

Pour répondre aux besoins de la presse mauricienne, pour combler les lacunes identifiées, des « formations » à la petite semaine, dispensées dans des conditions improvisées, ne feront plus l'affaire. Voilà pourquoi seule l'université peut se donner cette ambition en étroite collaboration avec la profession. Cette école pourrait avoir une vocation régionale. Les mêmes besoins existent dans les autres îles de la région. Il est possible d'imaginer la mobilisation de moyens financiers auprès des bailleurs de fonds étrangers, notamment européens, dans le cadre d'un projet régional.

Il va sans dire que la première responsabilité de former ses cadres appartient à l'entreprise. Jusqu'ici, sauf rares exceptions, les patrons de presse ont très peu investi dans la formation. Ils ont trouvé les moyens de financer l'achat de matériel de pointe pour produire des publications de bonne qualité technique, mais peu d'entreprises de presse prévoient un vrai budget de formation. Leur politique de recrutement est par ailleurs désastreuse.

Les conséquences de cette absence de vision commencent à se manifester. La qualité technique s'améliore, mais dans de nombreux cas, la qualité éditoriale baisse. Ces effets seront encore plus visibles dans quelques années, quand la petite dizaine de journalistes d'expérience se retireront. Ils ont les uns et les autres trente à quarante ans de métier, ils ont accompagné l'évolution du pays et même quand ils n'ont pas été formés dans les écoles de journalisme, ils ont largement compensé cette faiblesse par la studieuse acquisition d'une vaste culture générale. La relève est mal préparée.

Une question vient naturellement à l'esprit : les entreprises de presse sont- elles capables de payer à leur juste valeur des diplômés qui auraient fait des études universitaires doublées de longues années de formation professionnelle ? Pas toutes. Mais les journaux de qualité ne pourront se dispenser de journalistes de qualité. Déjà, les meilleurs professionnels de la presse sont à des niveaux de salaires tout à fait honorables, comparables à ceux des cadres supérieurs. Il y aura toujours quelques publications marginales, des « journaux » de complaisance ou de connivence qui opéreront dans une autre logique, mais les principaux titres de la presse nationale vont devoir se battre sur le terrain de la qualité professionnelle et de l'éthique.

Ce qui nous amène à la question cruciale de la rentabilité des entreprises de presse. Pour produire un journal de qualité, attirer et conserver les meilleurs professionnels, satisfaire les attentes exigeantes et diverses des lecteurs, garantir son indépendance éditoriale, il faut des investissements considérables et une rigoureuse gestion. Sur la douzaine de sociétés de presse du pays, seuls deux ou trois groupes sont actuellement rentables. On estime que pour un chiffre d'affaires global de plus de Rs 900 millions, les pertes d'exploitation (« opérationnelles ») de la presse mauricienne seront cette année de l'ordre de Rs 75 millions. Certains titres n'existent que grâce à un apport financier étranger, d'autres sont financés par des sources extérieures à l'entreprise elle-même, d'autres encore par des « parrains » anonymes. Les journaux indépendants sont ceux qui ne comptent que sur deux sources de revenus : les ventes et les recettes publicitaires. Et de manière générale, pour les produits grand public, les recettes publicitaires sont tributaires de l'étendue du lectorat.

Mais le marché de la presse commence à connaître des dysfonctionnements : d'une part, des journaux existent en défiant toute logique économique et commerciale grâce à des financements occultes ; d'autre part, le pouvoir politique fausse le jeu de la libre concurrence en utilisant les fonds publics pour subventionner des titres jugés bien-pensants et punir ceux qu'il considère comme trop critiques. C'est sans doute à ce niveau que se situe la plus grave menace pour la liberté de la presse écrite.

Le gouvernement semble vouloir affaiblir la presse dans son ensemble tout en ciblant certains titres en particulier. La paralysie voulue du Media Trust depuis plusieurs années illustre partiellement cette stratégie. Le Premier ministre a neutralisé le Media Trust en refusant de s'acquitter de son devoir, qui est de « appoint » le président du Trust. La profession n'a pas bronché.

Pourtant, créé par une loi adoptée en 1994, financé par l'Etat, dirigé par un conseil d'administration composé en majorité de professionnels de la presse, le Media Trust a rendu, en son temps, de grands services à la profession. Selon la loi, les « *objects* » du Trust sont clairement définis : « *a) to receive and manage funds obtained from government and other organisations ; b) to run a media and documentation centre ; c) to organise seminars, conferences, workshops and training courses ; d) to foster relations with the international media ; e) to carry out such other activities as the Board may decide.* »

C'est ainsi que le Media Trust a pu compter plusieurs réalisations marquantes : il a offert à la profession un centre polyvalent – salle de formation, salle de réunion et un musée photographique qui rend hommage à l'histoire de la presse mauricienne. Ce centre situé dans le vieux Port- Louis est aujourd'hui à l'abandon. Mais le plus notable, c'est la série de cours organisés régulièrement pendant des années avec la participation de formateurs mauriciens et étrangers, venus de Grande-Bretagne, des États- Unis ou de France. Des journalistes ont par ailleurs bénéficié de bourses offertes par le Trust pour suivre des formations assurées en France par l'École des Métiers de l'Information.

C'est également le Media Trust qui avait pris l'initiative de lancer le débat sur la nécessité de créer un organisme d'autorégulation de la profession, un *Press Council*. C'était en 1998. Avec le soutien de la Thomson Foundation, le conseil d'administration du Media Trust a confié à Kenneth Morgan, ancien directeur de la *British Press*

Complaints Commission, la tâche de proposer une formule adaptée aux réalités locales, mais en s'inspirant des meilleures pratiques des pays démocratiques. Ce consultant avait visité Maurice, rencontré un très large éventail de personnalités nationales de tous bords avant de formuler ses propositions dans un rapport intitulé *« A Press Council for Mauritius ? Safeguarding Freedom. Responsibility and Redress for Mauritius and its Media »* Kenneth Morgan a recommandé la création d'un *« Press Council »* sous l'égide d'un Media Trust Act réformé. Il s'agit d'un conseil volontaire chargé de *« preserving and defending press or media freedom as well as with maintaining high professionnal and ethical standards and with dealing with complaints." (Recommendation 47 3a).* A défaut d'un amendement de la loi, il a préconisé que les journalistes eux- mêmes, les propriétaires des entreprises de presse *« should themselves take the initiative in setting up a voluntary Press Council... »* Morgan a bien précisé que *« as a voluntary body, the council once set up and acknowledged by Parliament should be in charge of its own procedures and be seen so to be ." (Recommendation 48 3b).* Son rapport souligne de plus que *"media practitioners themselves should be responsible for drafting a code to be considered and ratified, possibly after amendment, by the new Press/Media Council."*

Malheureusement, ce besoin d'autorégulation n'avait alors pas fait l'unanimité dans la profession, parfois pour des raisons mesquines et des animosités personnelles, parfois par ignorance, parfois encore par arrogance intellectuelle, et le projet a été abandonné. C'est une erreur tragique et on a perdu beaucoup de temps.

Ce refus d'autorégulation a fait du tort à l'image de la presse. Elle est apparue comme orgueilleuse, exigeant la transparence de tous, mais refusant de s'appliquer les mêmes règles. Aujourd'hui, cette erreur est peut- être réparable. Une nouvelle association professionnelle, la *Newspaper Editors and Publishers Association (NEPA),* vient enfin de publier un code de déontologie. Il importe qu'il soit plus largement communiqué (la presse ne sait pas communiquer sur elle-même) et il faudrait surtout instituer une procédure de contrôle reconnue par les citoyens. Le rapport Morgan avait proposé que le président du Conseil de la presse soit une personnalité compétente sans lien avec la presse. Le président du Media Trust, les propriétaires des entreprises de presse, les journalistes, les membres de la société civile feraient partie de ce conseil.

Compte tenu de tous ces enjeux – le besoin de formation, les atteintes à la liberté de la presse, la nécessité d'une instance d'autorégulation reconnue par le pouvoir politique et la société civile –, il est devenu impératif de reconstituer le Media Trust. Les patrons de presse et les rédacteurs en chef devraient se réunir, désigner un président, et proposer sa nomination au Premier ministre. Par le passé, l'autorité politique a respecté le choix de la profession. C'est ce Media Trust renouvelé qui devrait être l'interlocuteur de l'Université de Maurice pour le projet de formation. Il sera de même le représentant de la profession auprès du gouvernement pour toute question intéressant l'ensemble de la presse, notamment la création d'une instance d'autorégulation reconnue par le Parlement. La difficulté sera de parvenir à trouver des règles de légitimation des représentants de la profession au sein d'un nouveau conseil d'administration. Ce ne sera pas simple dans un métier plus que jamais tiraillé par toutes sortes de divisions.

Il reste que malgré toutes ces insuffisances, malgré la campagne de dénigrement menée par le pouvoir politique, la presse demeure l'une des institutions les plus respectées des Mauriciens. J'ai toujours plaisir à citer Sydney Jacobson, ancien président d'un groupe de presse britannique devenu membre de la Chambre des lords, qui a dit lors d'un débat sur la presse *« My Lords, relations between politicians or the State and the Press have deteriorated, are deteriorating, and should on no account be allowed to… improve ! »* Il en sera ainsi.

24

Journalism and Training: Views of an insider

Henri Marimootoo
Senior Journalist at Week-End

By the time I was invited to take the floor at the winding-up session of the two-day seminar, nearly all the participants and panelists had already dug in the main theme (enhancing democracy) and the burden was laid on me to avoid repeating practically the same observations. But, *en passant*, let me say very briefly that I do not completely share the seemingly widespread fear that press freedom is under very serious attack in Mauritius. It is my view that the people of our country are so aware of the role of newspapers, radios, television, internet and other modern communication devices in a democratic society that no government here will never be able - nay allowed - to curtail press freedom. Attempts in the past have all failed. Whether those of the British conquerors during Adrien d'Epinay's pioneering period, during Second World War, in the 1960-70's under SSR's censorship or during the so-called economic decisive years of Sir Anerood Jugnauth. It is, as Junius rightly pointed out in the *Public Advertiser* as far back as 1769," as if it has been impressed upon our minds, instilled into our children, that the liberty of the press is a palladium of all the civil, political and religious rights..."

After all, if we want to be cynical, it is commonly known that if ever there should exist any will to subdue a newspaper, it is better to infiltrate its editorial room than to impose national laws which are sure then to be fiercely resisted and soon become counter-productive.

So, I shall seize this opportunity to opine on what I believe really need a bit more of my attention as a professional. I shall raise some questions about the training problems of the Mauritian journalist, the nature of journalism, its incompatibility with communication/PR and make, a least, one suggestion I think may help to protect the rights of citizens against abuses from the press itself...

Journalism and Communication/Public Relations

I was putting a final point to that presentation, last Friday, when - maybe it is mere coincidence - I received a phone call. A young voice went on with a resounding "Bonjour Monsieur Marimootoo! I am only calling to ask if I could have your name included in my contact book. I remember we once talked when you were sitting on the Board of the Media Trust in 2004, and thanks to that institution I was awarded a scholarship for a six-month training in journalism in Paris."

"Great ! And for which newspaper are you working now?" I asked because, as a matter of fact, I could not recall having come across his signature in any publication.

"No! I am no more in that field! Back in Mauritius, I spent only eight months in a newspaper but was very disappointed with the job. I very rapidly got tired of always reporting what others had to say without being myself allowed, even once, to have my views voiced. I am now the Press Attaché of Minister X. Could we keep in contact and communicate if need be?" For sure, I did not refuse. But, frankly, I could not help myself commenting that once against it's the same drama. I have seen so many young talented people quit the job never to return if not to come and go between editorial rooms and ministerial or corporate companies' press attaché's offices.

Mobility at work, freedom of choice to be or no more to be a journalist are not the only explanations why, in particular young journalists and reporters very often look for brighter prospects. There is a real problem !

As a journalist with a quite long career now, I feel ill at ease that more and more there seems to be no difference made nowadays between Journalism and Communication or Public Relations. To my view, making no difference at all and, worst of all, mixing courses like

174

Journalism-cum- Communication as does presently the University of Mauritius and some well-known private institutions is damaging the profession and does not favour in anyway enhancing a democratic society. Not very long ago, Ellen Hume, an American journalist who lectures around the world, came here to remind us about just two fundamental principles that spell about the elements of journalism:

(i) the first obligation of the journalist is to the truth even if it doesn't support his personal cause or his media sponsor. His first loyalty is to the citizens (the public).

(ii) whereas Public Relations and Marketing, in which a Press attaché is involved, are (I quote)" propaganda to promote the interests of those who contrive it, rather than to benefit those to whom it is addressed. Propaganda does not have to be true. It is deliberately biased. Sometimes totally false."

My explanation why some "journalists" do, *sans état-d'âme*, shift from truth to propaganda, lies in the following facts (i) they think, legitimately, that they can play a guiding role in society, but are not themselves free to comment (ii) they are under-paid and can easily be attracted by big packages which wealthy companies and ministers are ready to offer to cash in on their skills and (iii) some of them lack that training which confers confidence. But, is it not a real danger to democracy? When money can buy the best journalists who, instead of seeking the truth and publish it, turn to propagandists!

Training weaknesses of the Mauritian Press

First, it is no secret that journalism in Mauritius which goes back to 1834 has always been practised by autodidacts. Up to the 1970's, very few journalists could benefit from professional training . Thus, out of a staff of, say, ten journalists and reporters, only one or two could claim to have been professionally trained. They, in fact, were awarded scholarships to follow crash courses within British newspapers, Thomson Foundation or the journalism school of Berlin

175

(Germany). Then, their bosses had to rely on them to act as elder brothers helping the younger ones to do their homework. Fortunately, that system, sometimes one of trial and errors, worked because, above all, journalists and reporters of those times really wanted to break through a career. But, still there was greater need for more professionalisation.

Then came the Mauritius Media Trust which, by an Act of Parliament, instituted a quite interesting on-going training. The Mauritius Media Trust, well managed by elected members from the press itself did have some real success and, within ten years of existence, thirty-nine journalists and reporters were trained either at l'École des Métiers de la Communication in Paris or in Mauritius. It is to be emphasized that the Media Trust was generously assisted by the French and the American Embassies, the Friedrich Ebert Foundation, the British Council and the South African Development Community. But, and that was also its Achilles' heel; basically the funds came from the government! This situation explains why since 2005 the current Prime Minister, in his *"bras de fer"* with some local publications, thinks he is allowed to stall the activities of the Media Trust! It must also be noted that under the pretext that government funded the Media Trust some independent newspapers were reluctant to release their staff for courses as this could mean a kind of state control of the profession. At the end of the day, it is journalists and reporters who pay the price...

I am not willing to put the blame of the too little consideration for training entirely on the government. Clinically, the employers in the press business industry in Mauritius barely spend a cent for the training of their journalists and reporters. When they invest, it is only to ensure continuation in the payment of salaries or to provide some pocket money while their employees are abroad on scholarships sponsored by other institutions. Maybe also, occasionally, the services of foreign professional trainers are hired for in-house training by some newspapers or media groups, but in no way could these in-house coaching empower the journalists as would a diploma course from a recognised national or an international institution.

For redress, I would suggest the setting-up of either a Regional School of Journalism or l'École de Journalisme de l'Océan Indien et de l'Est-Afrique. In agreement with representatives of the professional body, the University of Mauritius could help pave the way. The school, which will have the main role of strengthening democracy in our part of the world, could be jointly funded by SADC member states (in line with their Windhöek Declaration (Namibia, 1980) to foster freedom of expression), Commonwealth Institutions, the European Commission, the UNDP, the Unesco, the Indian Ocean Commission, the Fonds d'Aide Européen pour la presse libre and Employers Associations. Employers need not make any additional financial contribution. Suffice it to ask for a re-allocation of the levy (around 2% of their annual turn-over) they already pay to the Human Ressouces Development Council (HRDC) which is left idle. But, while fund-providers could involve states, training programmes and syllabuses must, imperatively, be devised by local and regional professional journalists themselves with the assistance of European and American faculties. In any case, the diploma/master course must include an important investigative journalism specialization component. There lies the future of a really dynamic free press that could be a credible watch-dog and nation-builder.

Finally, my humble suggestion to deter malevolence and abuses from the press is only to extend the legal aid system to any individual, specially the down-trodden (*Ti dimunn*) who can prove he has enough ground to feel aggrieved by a press article.

25

Formation et Professionnalisme

Axcel Cheney
Journaliste à Radio Plus

Le texte qui suit est une transcription faite à partir d'un enregistrement audio de l'intervenant.

Nous avons un problème qui est beaucoup plus grave que ce que les éditorialistes écrivent tous les jours à chaque fois qu'il y une petite tension entre la presse et le pouvoir. On parle souvent de museler la presse, une atteinte à la liberté d'expression, la répression, la dictature anti-presse, etc. Mais je crois qu'il y un très gros problème de formation car il faut toujours tout refaire avec les nouvelles recrues car il manque toujours des points cruciaux à leur reportage. C'est un problème très grave. A qui la faute? La faute est à l'État quand il a arrêté de subventionner la formation et le perfectionnement des journalistes.

Les journalistes des années 1970/80/90 ont, eux, pu bénéficier des formations grâce à l'Ambassade de France et d'autres institutions.

Pour moi, cette année c'est ma première formation au CFPJ après huit années de service. Avant d'y aller, j'ai écrit au Media Trust. Le Media Trust ne finance pas la formation des journalistes qui veulent étudier ailleurs car ils n'ont qu'un budget administratif.

Pourquoi le secteur hôtelier a l'école hôtelière et pour les journalistes on a- t-on fermé la toute petite porte qui pouvait former des journalistes? C'est très barbare et rétrograde car on ne peut pas empêcher quelqu'un d'apprendre. C'est antidémocratique. Quelqu'un a dit récemment: « A qui profite le crime? »

Je pense sincèrement que ce sont les gouvernants qui profitent de ces situations:

• Il y d'abord un problème de forme. Un article peut être factuel, objectif, basé sur des faits, mais s'il est mal écrit, ça ne passe pas. Le rédacteur en chef le bloque.

• Ensuite, il y a un problème de fond. Quand un article qui dénonce est bien ficelé, solide, on a demandé de bonnes informations aux bonnes personnes, mais c'est surtout embarrassant pour le pouvoir. Quelquefois à cause de l'amateurisme et du manque de formation de certains de nos confrères, certaines dénonciations sont tombées pour des erreurs toutes bêtes (c'est comme pour les abus de procédure).

Il faut comprendre que les gouvernants ne vont pas nous aider à leur être plus embarrassants. Si le journal *Samedi Plus* révèle l'affaire Boskalis, croyez-vous que le Ministre de l'Information et Premier Ministre va donner une bourse au journaliste de *Samedi Plus*? « Je ne nourris pas le chien de la personne chez qui je vais aller voler .''
C'est un problème encore plus grave pour les radios privées et l'audiovisuel.

Le journaliste radio, c'est un journaliste complet qui doit connaître les techniques de prise de son. Il doit aller sur le terrain, ne pas avoir peur de se mouiller, doit savoir quelle personne interroger, doit avoir la notion de tournage. Tout est technique et journalistique.
Ce n'est pas quelqu'un qui du jour au lendemain devient journaliste radio. Il faut beaucoup d'expérience. Une rigueur s'impose au journaliste. Moi- même j'ai encore beaucoup à apprendre. Au CFPJ, j'ai admiré la rigueur qui s'impose au journaliste.
Imaginons qu'il y a une télé privée qui arrive chez nous, quel serait le profil du journaliste? Par exemple, chez France 24, il n'existe plus de cameraman, le Journaliste Reporter d'Images (JRI) s'occupe de la camera, de la prise se son, de l'interview et du montage jusqu'à la diffusion. Il est complet.
Il faut y ajouter toute la rigueur du journaliste de la presse écrite; il faut un bon carnet d'adresses, bien rempli, une rigueur déontologique, trouver l'information, comprendre son contexte et

maîtriser son sujet. Tout cela vient avec l'expérience. Or, les jeunes qui sortent de l'Université craquent souvent sous la pression du 16h30 à la radio. Ils ont besoin de plus de formation.

Il y a un gros souci pour le financement des formations des journalistes (un mois de formation au CFPJ coûte Rs 200,000), ce n'est pas facile et accessible à tout le monde. Or, le Media Trust ne finance plus. Il y a une urgence. Je fais d'ailleurs un appel aux employeurs.

Puisqu'on parle de démocratie, « une presse qui ne progresse pas contribue au recul de la démocratie »

Pour moi, Charles de Gaulle ne nous dira pas « Sois jeune et tais-toi ».

26

Formation et Professionnalisme

Jean-Luc Emile
Rédacteur en Chef à Radio One

Le texte qui suit est une transcription faite à partir d'un enregistrement audio de l'intervenant.

La presse est le poumon de la démocratie mais elle a ses défauts et ses qualités. Personne ne peut contester la légitimité de la presse qui est le chien de garde pour protéger la démocratie.

Il y a un regain d'intérêt pour la profession - c'est une presse qui s'est rajeunie. Mais il y un manque de rigueur – un renouvellement qualitatif et un réel renforcement des ressources humaines serait d'ailleurs bénéfique. Il y a certes une compétition entre les radios et la presse écrite qui ont les mêmes objectifs dans leurs viseurs. De fait, les journalistes d'aujourd'hui maîtrisent mieux les interventions plus précisément en direct.

Ce qu'on reproche cependant aux radios, c'est qu'il n'y a pas d'équilibre dans les interventions. Car ce sont les personnes mécontentes qui interviennent le plus souvent sur les ondes.

Or, les médias doivent participer à la socialisation du citoyen, qui est une noble mission mais avec de lourdes responsabilités: intellectuelles, professionnelles et aussi au niveau des compétences.

Les hommes politiques ne sont, eux, pas intéressés par la formation des journalistes - cette formation pour informer et éduquer. Les gouvernants devraient pourtant agir en avance et non pas quand les fautes ont été commises par les journalistes. Il faut éviter que ces fautes puissent arriver, il faut donc assurer plus de formations.

Les gouvernants devraient s'occuper plus de trouver des personnes qui pourraient venir à Maurice pour former les journalistes au lieu de trouver quelqu'un pour diriger une Media Commission pour sanctionner la presse.

Les gouvernants ont certes investi en créant le Media Trust - mais cet organisme n'a actuellement pas de conseil d'administration ni de président, il y a uniquement un bâtiment administratif, un président virtuel et un budget de Rs 2 millions qui n'est pas efficacement utilisé.

Bien sûr, il existe des stages avec l'appui des ambassades de France et des États-Unis mais cela comporte très peu d'échanges concrets. Les expériences dans des rédactions étrangères sont très importantes pour les journalistes.

Aujourd'hui les groupes de presse assurent eux-mêmes la formation et le perfectionnement des journalistes, mais cela coûte très cher, donc on ne peut envoyer plus d'une personne à la fois.

Radio One, Radio Plus, La Sentinelle, Le Defi-Media Group ont beaucoup investi – en faisant venir des étrangers même pour une courte période et cela coûte cher tout de même. Mais c'est très important pour assurer la qualité des produits, la qualité de l'antenne, le confort des auditeurs et aussi pour être en ligne avec la technologie informatique.

Le recrutement des journalistes qui n'ont pas vraiment de bases solides cause un problème grave. Sur le marché, il y a très peu de compétences, surtout pour la radio.

Surtout si la télévision privée arrive bientôt, il n'y aura pas les compétences requises sauf ceux qui sont à la MBC. C'est un challenge très important.

La HRDC, l'organisation qui doit s'assurer d'une meilleure qualité de ressources humaines se contente de rembourser à l'organisation de presse les coûts encourus pour les formations assurées. Mais elle n'a rien comme programme pour les jeunes qui veulent faire du journalisme.

Pour avoir une vraie formation, il faut donc s'inscrire à des universités payantes où les coûts sont exorbitants, de Rs 45,000 à Rs 50,000. Donc il faut plus de programmes de soutien, des bourses pour assurer plus de formations.

Le professionnalisme est un véritable challenge pour pouvoir garder ce rôle de chien de garde et peut être le chemin pour aller plus loin dans le rôle de quatrième pouvoir.

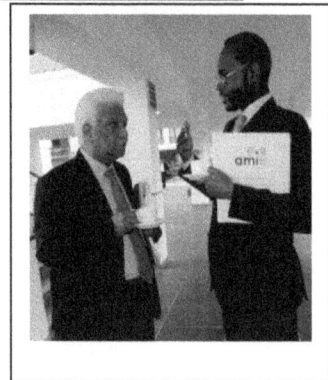

La démocratie au-delà du satisfecit convenu

Nazim ESOOF
09/14/10 | Commentaires [1]

Modifier la taille du texte: A|A

Commentaires   Noter l'article   Partager et classer cet article

SHARE

Dans le cadre de la Journée internationale de la démocratie, le 15 septembre, l'UoM organise une conférence sur le système démocratique et les médias à Maurice. Notre rapport à la démocratie demeure, toutefois, figé.

«*Tout est relatif. Si nous nous comparons à l'Afrique, nous pouvons dire que nous sommes bien avancés en termes de valeurs démocratiques. Mais, il y a plusieurs aspects du concept qui méritent d'être revus*», explique, d'emblée, Dan Bundhoo, membre de Democracy Watch Mauritius (DWM). «*Dans l'absolu, on retrouve une forme de démocratie assez avancée à Maurice. Mais, il reste pas mal de chemin à faire. Parfois, il y a des avancées, parfois, il y a des reculades*», note, dans la même veine, Christina Chan Meetoo, chargée de cours en communication à l'université de Maurice (UoM). «*A Maurice, il existe toutes les formes et structures de la démocratie. Mais dans le fonctionnement et la pratique, ce n'est pas tout à fait la réalité*», confi rme, de son côté, Jacques de Navacelle, directeur de Transparency International Mauritius et qui intervient en tant que citoyen.

Le constat est le même chez tous nos intervenants. Maurice peut s'enorgueillir de posséder les structures garantissant une démocratie vivante. Cependant, dans les faits, nous nous fi geons dans une forme d'immobilisme en termes d'aspirations démocratiques. Alors même que la démocratie, dans la défi nition qu'en donne les Nations unies, «*est un processus autant qu'un objectif, et seule la pleine participation et l'appui de la communauté internationale, des organes de gouvernance nationaux, de la société civile et des individus, permettront de faire de l'idéal démocratique une réalité universelle.*»

Nous sommes bien loin de cette dynamique démocratie. Qu'avons-nous fait de la démocratie ? Est-ce toujours, dans sa forme première telle que la conçoit le monde occidental, un système approprié pour des pays comme Maurice ? Quel est son poids réel face au néolibéralisme ?

Autant de questions que l'on doit se poser à la veille de cette Journée internationale. Il y a évidemment des motifs de satisfaction. «*Lorsqu'on regarde le monde autour de nous, on peut constater qu'il y a beaucoup de pays où la démocratie est en recul ou alors n'existe pas du tout*», rappelle, à cet effet, Jacques de Navacelle.

Si on ne peut pas parler de «*déficit ou de vide démocratique à Maurice*», il n'en demeure pas moins que le statu quo nous enfonce davantage dans des pratiques qui, tout en s'habillant de règles démocratiques, révèlent des intentionnalités et des ambitions antidémocratiques.

«*C'est clair qu'il existe une corruption de la démocratie à Maurice. Pour s'en sortir, il faudrait une réforme du système électoral afi n d'atténuer les lobbies fi nanciers et l'infl uence des lobbies sectaires sur la démocratie. Il faudrait donner plus de pouvoirs aux citoyens*», estime, en ce sens, le syndicaliste Ashok

UOM/UNESCO : Meeah, Deerpalsing et Obeegadoo parlent de presse et de démocratie

Estelle Bastien
09/15/10 | Commentaires [8]

Modifier la taille du texte: A｜A

Commentaires Noter l'article Partager et classer cet article

SHARE

L'Université de Maurice (UOM), en collaboration avec l'UNESCO organise deux jours de conférence sur les médias et la promotion de la démocratie à Maurice, le 16 et le 17 septembre. Le thème : *«Enhancing Democratic Systems: The Media in Mauritius»*.

Plusieurs parlementaires seront présents durant la session du 17 septembre, dont le député du Front Solidarité Mauricien (FSM), Cehl Meeah, la députée travailliste Nita Deerpalsing et Steven Obeegadoo du Mouvement militant mauricien (MMM).

Ils répondront aux questions de l'assistance sur les médias et les partis politiques.

Christina Chan-Meetoo, chargée de cours en communication à l'UOM, affirme que ces conférences sont l'occasion rêvée pour réunir tous les représentants des médias de Maurice et ceux des autorités. *«Nous avons voulu donner la chance à tout le monde de participer à cette plateforme pour justement promouvoir la démocratie et permettre le dialogue entre l'assistance et les dirigeants politiques»*, ajoute-t-elle.

Les représentants de chaque groupe de presse et de chaque formation politique ont été invités à participer à ces conférences. Cependant, en ce qui s'agit des partis politiques, Christina Chan-Meetoo fait ressortir qu'ils n'ont pas tous répondu à l'invitation.

Par ailleurs, les autres thèmes qui seront abordés lors de ces conférences sont : la MBC dans un secteur des médias en pleine évolution, les médias et les élections «Free and Fair» ou encore les radios privés au service du public et leurs intérêts commerciaux, entre autres.

L'accès à ces conférences est libre. D'ailleurs, l'UOM fait un appel aux Mauriciens pour qu'ils soient nombreux à y assister.

Workshop puts media under the microscope

By Sunil Gopal

The Mauritian media has come in for its fair share of criticism in recent days, with charges of stirring communal feelings, inaccuracy and downright misreporting.

Prime Minister Navin Ramgoolam has been at the forefront of the attacks and has pledged to introduce tough new media laws.

This backdrop will surely add "spice" to a two-day dialogue session with the theme "Enhancing Democratic Systems: The Media in Mauritius", staring today and organised by UNESCO in collaboration with the Media/Communication Unit of the University of Mauritius.

The opening session will be marked by the speech of the CEO of the African Media Initiative, Mr Amadou Mahtar Ba.

The first session today, to be chaired by Mr Ibrahim Khoduruth from the University of Mauritius, will focus on "freedom, media and democracy".

On Friday, session two, focusing on "media systems and policies" will be chaired by Mr Ba.

The theme of media, politics and democracy will be discussed during session three chaired by Mrs Sheila Bunwaree from the University of Mauritius. Part of the discussion will focus on "mainstream political parties and the media".

Leader of Front Solidarité Mauricienne (FSM) Cehl Meeah, the MMM secretary general (international relations) Steve Obeegadoo and the director of communications of the Mauritius Labour Party, Miss Nita Derpalsing, will be the main speakers during this discussion.

Session four — citizens and the media — will be chaired by Mrs Caroline Ng Tseung Wong from the University of Mauritius.

The fifth and last session will focus on "challenges to the journalism trade: training and professionalism", and will be chaired by Mrs Christina Chan Meetoo from the university.

"You will no doubt concur with us that the thematic is both timely and pertinent in light of recent exchanges and debates concerning the state of media on our island as well as the different bodies and systems linked to it," said Miss Roukaya Kasenally and Mrs Christina Chan Meetoo, the conveners of the dialogue session.

The main objectives of the workshop are:

● Take stock of the existing battery of legal and regulatory framework with respect to the media in Mauritius
● Revisit the various debates/exchanges about the changing role of the media in a democracy
● Examine the relationship between the media and the different institutions such as the government, regulatory bodies and civil society
● Explore the good practices available in the area of media regulation/self-regulation
● Engage in dialogue with key stakeholders in relation to the above and ensure a way forward for prompt implementation.

"As for the various sessions, they will explore issues pertaining to governance, freedom and democracy, regulation, public service and commercial broadcasting, elections and democracy, citizenship and the media among others," explained the conveners.

"Through this dialogue, we also hope to build upon existing work already done such as the 2008 UNESCO-IPDC Media Development Indicators or the 2008 African Barometer report for Mauritius and to synergise efforts towards an enhanced democratic system that strikes the right balance between freedom of information or expression and media governance," stated the conveners.

African media guru

● Mr Amadou Mahtar Ba is the chief executive of the African Media Initiative (AMI), a pan-African effort aimed at providing the continent's media owners and practitioners with the tools they need to play an effective role in their societies.

AMI aims to strengthen the media sector in Africa to ensure the accountability of governments and other institutions and to promote social development and economic growth.

Mr Ba is also a co-founder and president of All Africa Global Media, Inc, an international multimedia content service provider, systems technology developer and the largest distributor of African news and information worldwide.

He is a member of the World Economic Forum's Global Council for the Future of Journalism, advisory board member of the Reporting Developing Network Africa, as well as a member of the Advisory Committee of the Knight International Journalism Fellowship administered by the International Center for Journalists (ICFJ).

Mr. Ba was educated in Senegal, France and Spain and is multilingual.

190

L'express 17/09/2010

Presse-pouvoir : Appel à un débat franc à l'université de Maurice de Amadou Mahtar Ba

Estelle Bastien
09/17/10 | Commentaires [0]

"Enhancing Democratic Systems:
The Media in Mauritius".

16th & 17th September 2010
ELT2 Engineering Tower, UOM

| Modifier la taille du texte: | A ∣ A | | Commentaires | Noter l'article | SHARE Partager et classer cet article |

«Il ne faut surtout pas se crisper». C'est ce qu'a affirmé, hier jeudi 16 septembre, Amadou Mahtar Ba, directeur général de l'African Media Initiative (AMI) qui participe à une conférence organisée par l'Université de Maurice (UoM), en collaboration avec l'UNESCO. Ce dernier se dit avoir observé la situation entre les médias et la politique à Maurice, et il conseille qu'il y ait un «débat franc» entre les deux.

«Il y a une situation assez tendue entre les médias et la politique, à Maurice. Mais c'est une situation qui arrive souvent dans d'autres pays également. Cependant je pense qu'il faut que les deux parties en conflit discutent de façon claire, avoir un débat franc pour le bien de la population mauricienne», affirme le directeur général de l'AMI.
Par ailleurs, Amadou Mahtar Ba, estime que les médias ne devraient pas être se lier à un parti politique en particulier. Cependant, si des formations politiques ont leurs propres médias, le directeur de l'AMI soutient qu'il devrait également avoir de la place pour les médias privés, toujours pour le bien de la population.

De plus, durant cette première journée de conférence, plusieurs membres des différents groupes de presse ont pris la parole sur des thèmes bien spécifiques. Ainsi, Subash Gobine, du groupe Défi, a affirmé qu'il n'y avait pas que les dirigeants politiques qui empêchent les médias de bien faire leur travail, mais aussi les organisations privées, notamment, celles dites «socioculturelles».

Gilbert Ahnee de La Sentinelle, a, quant à lui, préféré mentionner la responsabilité du journaliste à rester honnête, loin de la corruption. «Maurice n'est pas une dictature, la presse peut jouir de liberté». Cependant, il affirme aussi que cette liberté ne suffit pas que le journaliste doit se montrer responsable.

Pour rappel, il y a aura une deuxième session de conférence, ce vendredi 16 septembre. Les interventions seront axées sur le système des médias, les citoyens et les médias ainsi que sur la politique et les médias, avec les interventions des représentants de plusieurs formations politiques.

L'express 17/09/2010

Conférence à l'UoM : Accent sur la presse libre pour la sauvegarde de la démocratie

Estelle Bastien
09/17/10 | Commentaires [11]

Modifier la taille du texte: A | A

Commentaires   Noter l'article   SHARE

Partager et classer cet article

Dans le cadre de la conférence sur les médias à Maurice, organisé par l'Université de Maurice et l'UNESCO, plusieurs membres de formations politiques sont intervenus, aujourd'hui, 17 septembre. Présidé par Sheila Bunwaree, chargée de cours à l'UoM, cette séance était largement axée sur les relations conflictuelles entre la politique et les médias.

Le leader du Front solidarité mauricien, Cehl Meeah, Steeve Obeegadoo du Mouvement militant mauricien, Nita Deerpalsing, du Parti travailliste, Ashok Subron de Rezistans & Alternativ et Nilen Vencadasamy du Blok 104 ont, à tour de rôle, fait valoir leur appréciation du rôle de la presse mauricien par rapport aux politiques.

Cehl Meeah a appelé à ne pas publier des informations qui risqueraient de trouble la paix sociale, précisant que «*les journaux ne doivent jamais écrire ce qui trouble le peuple*». Mais il estime aussi que la presse doit pouvoir fonctionner en toute liberté et dans le respect des lois. Le leader du Front solidarité mauricien soutient que l'Etat «*ne doit pas contrôler la presse d'une façon abusive*».

De son côté, Steeve Obeegadoo a fustigé le rôle de la Mauritius Broadcasting Corporation (MBC) pendant la dernière campagne électorale. «L'opposition continue à dire que les résultats des élections ont été faussés par la MBC», a dit le député du Mouvement militant mauricien (MMM). Il considère qu'alors que «*la population a droit à l'information*», la MBC se contentait de ne couvrir «*que ce qu'elle considérait favorable au gouvernement sortant*».

Steeve Obeegadoo, revenant sur les remarques des membres du gouvernement contre la presse, soutient que «*plutôt que des menaces contre la presse tous les jours, il faut voir ce qui se passe ailleurs*». «*Gouvernement et presse doivent trouver un terrain d'entente*», ajoute le député mauve, car il faut une presse libre et démocratique. «*Gare au monopole, a-t-il ajouté. Cela d'autant plus qu'une presse démocratique est le reflet de toutes les facettes de la société mauricienne.*»

De son côté, Nita Deerpalsing a lancé que «*tout comme parmi les politiciens, dans la presse également il y a des pourris*». Et de se lancer dans une série de virulentes critiques contre La Sentinelle, insistant sur le fait que ce groupe de presse est très proche de certains secteurs socio-économiques précis.

Ashok Subron, de Rezistans & Alternativ, a fait ressortir, pour sa part, que c'est grâce aux medias que les groupes politiques extra-parlementaires ont pu se faire connaître et conscientiser la population sur l'importance de leur combat contre le communalisme. Pour lui, la presse ne doit jamais se soumettre au diktat de l'Etat. Il sera rejoint dans ses propos par Nilen Vencadasamy, qui a exprimé sa reconnaissance à l'express-dimanche pour avoir fait connaître l'action des militants qui avait pris position contre le communalisme au moment de l'enregistrement des candidats pour les élections.

Il n'a pas manqué de saluer le journaliste de l'express Nad Sivaramen qui a été le premier à utiliser le terme Blok 104, pour les 104 aspirants candidats refusant de décliner leur appartenance communale pour les élections de 2010.

192

Media should 'regulate self'

APOLOGY, CORRECTION MORE EFFECTIVE THAN LEGAL SANCTION SAYS EXPERT

By Sunil Gopal

The CEO of the African Media Initiative, Mr Amadou Mahtar Ba, said yesterday that self-regulation by the media is the best option.

He insisted that a self-regulatory body headed by an Ombudsperson is far more efficient than a statutory body.

Mr Ba was speaking at the opening of the dialogue session on "Enhancing Democratic Systems: The Media in Mauritius" at the University of Mauritius.

The dialogue session is jointly organised by the University of Mauritius and UNESCO.

"It is more appropriate that an Ombudsperson of a self-regulatory body address a complaint by urging for an apology and a correction from the media rather than a legal sanction from a statutory body.

"Apology and correction are more effective as it would entail that the publication has been either inaccurate or unprofessional, or both. This will affect its credibility and is a more ultimate sanction than a legal one," he said.

He added that self-regulation should not left in the hands of the media alone. He suggested that people from other sectors but familiar with the media be taken on board.

He also explained that there is no recipe for getting the media practitioners to group together as everything depends on every country's specificities.

"There must be some luminary who could give a push to grouping the media and make all understand that there are numerous challenges ahead," said Mr Ba.

He expressed concern about the tendency in some advanced countries on the African continent like South Africa, Kenya and Senegal to move away from media self-regulatory bodies to statutory bodies.

"My biggest fear is the domino effect," he said.

Asked about the conflicting situation between the government and the media in Mauritius, Mr Ba replied that this type of situation arises when a political leader has the impression that a particular media organisation is against him. He added that in the long run both politicians and media practitioners are accountable to the population.

"There cannot be a totally appeased relation between politicians and the media," said Mr Ba.

Earlier he explained that the media is one of the most important facets of democracy anda should however be free, independent, ethical and professional.

"Democracy needs a vibrant parliament, a dynamic private sector and also an independent media," said Mr Ba.

The Acting Pro-Chancellor of the University of Mauritius, Assistant Professor Daneshwar Puchooa said he hoped that the sessions of the conference will help building dialogues between the media and other stakeholders.

The Dean of the Faculty of Social Studies and Humanities Sanjeev Kumar Sobhee expressed the wish that the conference provides the opportunity of a heated debate on media and democracy.

The conference concludes today

Le Défi 18/09/2010

Médias - Quand la régulation de la presse fait débat

Analyser les relations de la presse avec le pouvoir. «Une presse libre et indépendante est la racine meme d'une bonne démocratie». C'est ce qu'a lancé d'emblée, Amadou Mahtar Ba, Chairman de l'African MediaInitiative, lors du débat organisé à l'Université de Maurice, jeudi.

« Ce sujet fait non seulement débat à Maurice, mais également sur tout le Continent noir», a assuré le CEO tout au long de son exposé. Il est allé encore plus loin en affirmant que les médias « sont un des piliers d'une bonne économie, d'une bonne société, ainsi que d'une bonne démocratie».

«L'avancée, le développement de l'Afrique, dépend énormément d'une bonne presse libre et indépendante » a également indiqué Amadou Mahtar Ba. «C'est d'ailleurs ce qu'a affirmé le président des États-Unis dans un de ses discours. Barack Obama avait reconnu que le succès de l'Afrique dépend de la liberté de la presse," a poursuivi Amadou Mahtar Ba. Abordant les relations presse/pouvoir, le CEO de l'African Media Initiative a estimé que les médias sont l'oxygène de la politique. «Pour avoir une bonne démocratie, il faut que ces deuxparties parviennent à comprendre qu'ils sont tous deux redevables envers l'opinion publique». Amadou Mahtar Ba s'est également exprimé sur les intentions (avouées) du gouvernement mauricien de venir réglementer le monde des médias à Maurice. Un organe d'autorégulation serait préférable. Le gouvernement mauricien devrait mettre sur pied un «self regulatory body ," au lieu d'un organe de contrôle ('suprematory body'). L'organe d'autorégulation devra comprendre des gens issus de la presse, ainsi que d'autres membres indépendants. Ils leur reviendront de juger, de déterminer si les journalistes et autres membres de la profession ont fauté dans l'exercice de leurs fonctions," a-t-il indiqué. «Dans ce cas, si le titre de presse a réellement fauté, il devra présenter des excuses et demander pardon», a-t-il ajouté. «Une telle initiative prouvera que dans la rédaction de son article, le journaliste a été malhonnête, et a agi de manière non professionnelle. Il n'y a pas pire sanction pour un média. Le fait de dire à son audience qu'on a commis une erreur, c'est, selon moi, un aveu qui risque de lui coûter cher. Si le lecteur vouait une confiance totale en ce titre de presse, ce ne sera désormais plus le cas. Le lecteur commencera à se poser des questions. Et si le lecteur n'a plus confiance dans un titre de presse, le média en question ne pourra plus exister.

N'oublions pas que le lecteur est le juge suprême des médias».

Selon l'intervenant, forcer les médias qui ont fauté à payer des amendes, ne servira à rien, «car si un groupe de presse a les moyens de payer ces amendes, il continuera à opérer et à commettre d'autres fautes sans gêne aucune», a conclu Amadou Mahtar Ba.

Interventions

Maneesh Gobin : Lors de son intervention, le consultant légal Maneesh Gobin a dressé un sombre tableau de la Fonction publique qui, selon lui, opère dans l'opacité. «Je trouve malhonnête que les fonctionnaires tentent constamment de bloquer l'information aux membres du public." Il a fait référence à la pratique en vigueur dans la Grande Péninsule. «Depuis plusieurs années, l'Inde a senti le besoin d'agir dans la transparence, en rendant publiques toutes les activités impliquant l'argent du contribuable». D'où la nécessité d'introduire le Freedom of Information Act. Gilbert Ahnee : Le président de la News Editor Papers Association a déploré que des groupes privés « mettent en marche de grosses opérations pour corrompre les journalistes." Selon Gilbert Ahnee, lorsqu'on évoque les groupes privés, «il faut aussi inclure les organisations non gouvernementales qui disposent de gros moyens financiers et qui mettent tout en oeuvre pour acheter l'intégrité des journalistes. C'est pourquoi, il revient à chaque journaliste d'assumer ses responsabilités.»

Subash Gobine : Le consultant du Defi Media Group a rappelé les divers événements qui prouvent cette relation si tendue entre la presse et le pouvoir. Il a cité notamment l'arrestation de deux journalistes pour avoir empiété un terrain privé. À une question de Christina Chan Meetoo, chargée de cours à l'Université, qui l'interrogeait sur l'état d'esprit des journalistes face aux menaces constantes du Premier ministre de museler les médias, Subash Gobine répond «Nous n'éprouvons aucune crainte. J'ai assisté dans le passé à des événements beaucoup plus sombres. Si la presse mauricienne a survécu à toutes ces menaces, cela prouve bien que le monde des médias a énormément mûri chez nous," assure-t- il.

The Independent 19/09/2010

WORLD: **PAGE 5**
BIRMINGHAM: POPE BEATIFIES ANGLICAN CONVERT

SPORTS: **PAGE 13**
CYCLING: NIBALI ON COURSE TO FIRST EVER GRAND PRIX

MAGAZINE: **PAGE 16**
RAVISHING RAIMA: THE ACTOR ON DOING OFFBEAT ROLES

the Independent

VOL 1, NO 266, PORT LOUIS, MONDAY, SEPTEMBER 20, 2010   10 PAGES   RS 10

DAILY

Meet emphasises independence of media

Independent News Service
Réduit, September 19

The media plays a crucial role in society and it includes the print media, radio, television and the Internet. It has become an important tool that can support or denounce the government and to voice the grievances of the people.

The managing director of the African Media Initiative (AMI), Amadou Ba Mahtar participated in a seminar organised by the University of Mauritius (UoM), in collaboration with the UNESCO, on Thursday. He said that both the public and private media has its importance in society since it helps to strike a balance.

"We cannot build a country, hoping that it is rooted in democracy if there is only one type of media. By definition, I think the media should be independent of political parties, although this doesn't seem to be the case in several countries," said Mahtar.

He added that he was aware of a situation on the island which is "not at all ideal that prevails in the country." He explained his point and emphasised that politicians and the media honchos must re-

Managing director of 'African Media Institute', Amadou Ba Mahtar speaks at a seminar held by UOM in collaboration with UNESCO on Thursday

alise that it is important to come and discuss on the ways to improve the lives of citizens.

Mahtar also said: "I look forward to the situation easing in Mauritius. There is no need to antagonise or personalise our differences. We must maintain an open dialogue so that people can benefit," said the managing director.

However, he said that he did

not expect a utopian situation to prevail among the media and politics.

"Although we speak in a frank manner, we cannot expect a state of utopia to prevail. There will always be differences between the media and political power. It is the nature of business," said Mahtar. The managing director said that a solution can lead to an

agreement between the two professions and urged "people of the media and politicians call for a frank discussion. You have to make compromises because the well-being of the population relies on it," said Mahtar.

Lawyer Maneesh Gobin spoke on the opportunities and constraints of the media industry. Abdollah Erally on his part spoke on the role of private radio. Roukaya Kasenally lecturer at the UoM discussed the theme '21st Century Broadcasting: The need to revisit and reinvent established systems'.

MPs Nita Deerpalsing, Steven Obeegadoo and Cehl Meeah spoke on "Mainstream Political Parties and the Media." Rabin Bhujun, editor of the l'Express Dimanche and Avinash Meetoo, meanwhile, raised the subject of "Advent of Digital Content: Experiments in Online Journalism."

A round table was chaired by Christina Chan Meetoo where Kiran Ramsahye editor of Le Matinal, Ariane Cavalot of Estrac Henry Marimootoo, Axcel Cheney discussed the issue of 'Challenges to the Trade Journalism: Training and Professionalism'.

feedback@theindependent.mu

197

Le Matinal

Vol VII, No 10, Port-Louis

P15

Iran

H. Clinton s'inquiète d'une dérive militaire

La secrétaire d'Etat américaine Hillary Clinton a souhaité que des leaders "responsables" prennent le contrôle d'un Etat iranien dont elle estime qu'il est de plus en plus sous la coupe des militaires. "Je ne pourrais espérer qu'il y aura un effort en Iran de la part de leaders civils et religieux responsables pour prendre le contrôle de l'appareil d'Etat", a-t-elle dit

DARING STAR

P11

CANCELLARA LIBÉRÉ

"L'INNOVATION REPRÉSENTE LE MOT-CLÉ DE LA COMPÉTITIVITÉ" : DINA JEETAH P6   Visit : www.lematinal.com

▌CONFÉRENCE

"Médias et politique, ménage possible grâce au dialogue"

BHAVNA FULENA
Port-Louis, 19 septembre

QU'ILS SOIENT publics ou privés, les médias jouent un rôle crucial dans une société. Regroupant la presse, la radio, la télévision, l'Internet, les mass media sont devenus des vecteurs importants qui peuvent faire ou défaire un gouvernement, en dénoncer ses abus, aussi bien que donner la parole au petit peuple.

Amadou Mahtar Ba, directeur général de l'African Media Initiative (AMI) participait à une conférence organisée par l'Université de Maurice, en collaboration avec l'UNESCO, jeudi et vendredi, a déclaré que les media publics et privés ont leur raison d'être dans une socie-té, car cela aide à maintenir un équilibre raisonnable. "Nous ne pouvons construire un pays, espérant qu'il soit ancré dans la démocratie s'il y a seulement un seul type de média. Il est important de diversifier. Par définition, j'estime que les médias ne doivent pas être rattachés à un parti politique, bien que cela semble être un fait normal dans plusieurs pays", a déclaré le directeur général de l'AMI au Matinal.

Parlant sur les mass media à Maurice, notre interlocuteur dit avoir pris connais-sance d'une situation "pas du tout idéale qui règne dans le pays". Expliquant cette opinion, il a tenu à faire ressortir que les politiciens et ceux responsables des médias doivent prendre conscience qu'il est du devoir de chacun de venir autour d'une table et discuter, pour améliorer la vie des citoyens. Pour Amadou Mahtar Ba, vivre dans une situation de décrispation ne sert à rien dans une société qui se déclare être une démocratie. "J'attends vivement une situation de décrispation à l'île Maurice. Il n'y a pas lieu d'antagonismes ou de personnalisations de différences. Il faut maintenir un dialogue ouvert, afin que le peuple puisse en bénéficier" a-t-il ajouté. Toutefois, se disant réaliste, le directeur de l'AMI affirme ne pas attendre qu'une situation d'utopie y règne entre le secteur médiatique et la politique. "Bien que nous parlions d'une façon franche et directe, nous ne pouvons nous attendre à une situation d'utopie. Il y aura toujours des divergences entre les médias et le pouvoir politique.

C'est la nature même des deux professions", a lancé le conférencier. Une solution pour venir à un accord entre ces deux professions, a conseillé notre interlocuteur, est "que les gens des médias et les politiciens préconisent un débat franc. Il faut faire des compromis, car le bien être de la population doit rester le but crucial des deux parties", a fait ressortir Amadou Mahtar Ba.

Parmi les thèmes discutés durant cet atelier de travail à l'UoM qui regroupait des char-=gés de cours, des journalistes et rédacteurs en chef, nous retrouvons l'intervention de l'avocat Maneesh Gobin, basé sur "les opportunités et les contraintes de l'industrie médiatique". Abdoolah Earally qui a, pour sa part, parlé du rôle des radios privées. Roukaya Kasenally, chargée de cours à l'UoM a évoqué le thème "21st Century Broadcasting: The need to revisit and reinvent esta-blished systems". Les députés de l'Assemblée nationale, Cehl Meeah, Steven Obeega-doo et Nita Deerpalsing ont, de leur côté, parlé sur le thè-me "Mainstream Political Parties and the Media". Rabin Bhujun, rédacteur en chef de l'Express Dimanche et Avinash Meetoo ont, quant à eux, abordé le sujet "Advent of Digital Content : Expe-riences in Online Journa-lism". Une table ronde, présidée par Christina Chan Meetoo a réuni Kiran Ramsahye, rédacteur en chef du Matinal, Ariane Cavalot de l'Estrac du groupe La Sentinelle, Henri Marimootoo de Week-End, Axel Cheney de Radio One, qui ont débattu sur le thème "Challenges to the Journalism Trade : Training and Profes-sionalism". – bhavna.f@lematinal.mu

Amadou Mahtar Ba : «La sanction pour un media ne peut venir que du citoyen»

Gilles RIBOUËT
09/21/10 | Commentaires [1]

Modifier la taille du texte: A | A

Commentaires   Noter l'article

SHARE

Partager et classer cet article

Invité du département de communication de l'université de Maurice, Amadou Mahtar Ba est président de l'«African Media Initiative» et cofondateur d'«AllAfrica.com». Il rappelle qu'au final, c'est le lecteur qui est seul juge des dérapages de la presse.

En quoi la presse participe-t-elle des pratiques de bonne gouvernance ?

Il faut garder à l'esprit que les médias en général ont historiquement un rôle qui leur permet d'exposer les pratiques ou les faits des gouvernants politiques et économiques. Exposer est la première fonction.

La seconde consiste à aller derrière l'information. La fonction d'analyse, d'interprétation, de mise en perspective est essentielle. Dans tout système, il est important d'avoir des gens, en l'occurrence des professionnels, capables de dire et de critiquer de manière constructive l'action des gouvernants.

Souvent, les gouvernants sont agacés – et c'est un euphémisme – quand ils sont critiqués. Pensez-vous que cela améliore la gouvernance ?

S'ils ont constamment conscience qu'il y a des médias indépendants, professionnels et respectant une éthique, qui veillent et analysent leurs paroles, leurs actions, c'est là un moyen de les contraindre ou de les motiver à faire toujours mieux. Il n'y a rien de pire qu'une situation de pouvoir sans veille, sans garde-fous. Les médias sont ces garde-fous dont l'influence est bénéfique pour la promotion des bonnes pratiques politiques et économiques. Mais, pour que la fonction des médias soit effective, il faut qu'ils soient formés et qu'ils observent une éthique professionnelle.

L'éthique sous-tend la régulation. De qui doit venir cette régulation ?

A mon avis, la meilleure formule est celle de l'autorégulation. Bien entendu, cette autorégulation doit être ouverte, consensuelle et inclusive. Si, par exemple, se constitue une commission de régulation des médias, il ne faut pas qu'elle soit uniquement composée de journalistes et professionnels des médias. Il faut l'ouvrir à des représentants de la société civile, voire des représentants du gouvernement. Il ne faut pas, je pense, tomber dans le travers d'une régulation des médias par les pouvoirs publics. Cela ne pourra engendrer qu'une polarisation et ce sont les citoyens du pays qui en souffriront au final. La pluralité, la diversité et l'indépendance de l'information sont nécessaires aux citoyens et ne peuvent être garanties que par une régulation venant des professionnels eux-mêmes.

On dit des médias qu'ils constituent le quatrième pouvoir. Certains les incorporent à la société civile. Quel est le rôle des médias ?

Les médias doivent exercer un rôle d'information et de garde-fous des gouvernants et politiques d'une part, du secteur privé et des acteurs de la société civile d'autre part. Donc, on ne peut pas dire que les médias appartiennent à la société civile. Ils ont un statut à part. Ils représentent effectivement ce qu'on appelle le quatrième pouvoir, compte tenu de leur influence, de leurs analyses et des informations qu'ils présentent. Leur fonction de transmission et d'analyse des informations participent de la bonne marche démocratique d'un pays.

Pourtant, à Maurice, il est arrivé, même très récemment, qu'on mette des bâtons dans les roues à cette bonne marche démocratique, à coups de boycott, de diatribes enflammées ou de flammes réelles...

Le Défi/L'Hebdo 26/09/2010

Relations tendues entre la presse et le pouvoir :Une rencontre avec le Premier ministre souhaitée

L'apaisement ! Tel est le souhait de la presse par rapport au conflit qui l'oppose au pouvoir. Samedi, dans l'émission Pour ou Contre, sur Radio Plus, le député et journaliste Reza Issack a accepté la proposition de Nawaz Noorbux d'agir comme une courroie de transmission entre la presse et le Premier ministre. Sa mission première sera de convaincre Navin Ramgoolam d'accepter une rencontre avec la presse pour mettre les points sur les i et tirer un certain nombre de choses au clair.

Outre Reza Issack, les invités étaient : Jean- Claude de l'Estrac, Subash Gobine, l'avocat Manish Gobin et la chargée de cours Christina Chan-Meetoo. Les trois représentants de la presse sont unanimes à dire que cette situation conflictuelle n'est pas nouvelle. Tout comme les menaces contre la presse ne le sont pas ! De tout temps et dans toute démocratie, le pouvoir pense être injustement critiqué par la presse. À Maurice, les réactions ont toujours été dures. Comme le dépeint Jean-Claude de l'Estrac : «Ramgoolam père est allé jusqu'à instaurer la censure et emprisonner des journalistes. Sous sir Anerood Jugnauth, il y a eu des tentatives pour asphyxier la presse d'un point de vue économique. Quand Paul Bérenger était Premier ministre, il avait présidé une réunion du Cabinet au cours de laquelle la décision a été prise de mettre sur pied un comité, comprenant Alan Ganoo et Ivan Collendavelloo, visant à serrer la vis aux radios privées. »

Jean-Claude de l'Estrac flaire un danger pour la presse. D'abord, dit-il, le gouvernement se sert de la manne publicitaire pour favoriser certains titres et en asphyxier d'autres. Ensuite, depuis cinq ans, le Premier ministre a paralysé le Media Trust en ne nommant pas de président. De plus, Navin Ramgoolam menace de venir de l'avant avec des lois contraignantes, notamment la mise sur pied d'une Media Commission.

Reza Issack, lui, ne voit aucun danger se profiler à l'horizon. « Je ne suis pas d'accord lorsque vous dites que le gouvernement a une stratégie visant à asphyxier la presse. Il n'y a aucune tentative de museler la presse. Il faut bien comprendre que le Premier ministre n'est pas contre la presse, mais contre la publication des fausses nouvelles », explique-t-il.

Pour le député et journaliste, la présente réaction du gouvernement fait suite à certaines actions de la presse. Il dit qu'il ne faut pas regarder qu'une face de la médaille. «Certains reprochent au gouvernement de cibler une section de la presse. Le contraire aussi est vrai. Une certaine presse cible le gouvernement. Certains, au sein du gouvernement, ont l'impression qu'une section de la presse s'acharne contre eux ," lance-t-il. Pour preuve, il cite un article de presse faisant état d'un incident à Vallée-Pitot entre le vice-Premier ministre, Rashid Beebeejaun, et un de ses mandants. « J'étais sur place. Le journaliste n'était pas là. Il a écrit son papier à partir des échos alors qu'il n'y a pas eu d'incident. C'est de la désinformation ," déplore-t-il. Il rend aussi la presse responsable de certaines manipulations :

« Pendant la campagne électorale, un journal a publié deux photos de deux foules, prises sous deux angles différents. Pour un parti, la photo expose bien la foule. Alors que, pour l'autre parti, la photo prise, à partir de l'estrade, montre une foule clairsemée. Cela joue sur l'imagination et les nerfs des gens. Vous devez donc vous attendre à des réactions.»

Subash Gobine ne croit pas que le gouvernement puisse enrayer les acquis de la presse. En revanche, il s'attend à une amélioration du niveau journalistique avec l'arrivée des nouveaux médias.

Discrimination dans la répartition des publicités

Jean-Claude de l'Estrac s'est plaint du boycott publicitaire gouvernemental dont fait l'objet le groupe La Sentinelle. Il a révélé que la fermeture du robinet publicitaire par le gouvernement, les corps paraétatiques et les firmes proches du Premier ministre engendrent un manque à gagner de Rs 20 millions par an. « Si nous n'avions pas diversifié nos activités, notre groupe aurait disparu ," a-t-il déclaré. Il est persuadé que son groupe remportera une victoire légale sur le gouvernement. Il a également fait une sortie contre les intérêts des financiers dans la presse. Subash Gobine et Reza Issack se sont, eux, intéressés au revers de la médaille. Le secteur privé, ont-ils dit, pratique également la discrimination dans la répartition de leurs publicités. Certaines grosses firmes boycottent carrément certains titres. Ils ont appelé à l'équité à tous les niveaux.

Une Media Commission

L'institution d'une Media Commission portera un coup à l'image de Maurice sur le plan international. Christina Chan-Meetoo, chargée de cours à l'université de Maurice, prévient que Maurice va chuter dans plusieurs classements internationaux.

«Il faut un minimum de régulation par l'état. L'autorégulation est plus importante. C'est une occasion pour la presse de s'unir et de venir de l'avant avec un mécanisme," suggère-t-elle. L'avocat Manish Gobin estime que la Media Commission sera une bonne chose si elle aide les citoyens à obtenir réparation pour des torts commis par la presse. Cependant, il n'est pas en faveur de son utilisation pour restreindre la liberté des journalistes.

Il soutient qu'il existe suffisamment de lois à Maurice pour sanctionner les journalistes qui ont fauté.

Dans cette même veine, il a proposé que la diffamation soit décriminalisée. « En Angleterre, on vient de le faire. Il n'est pas possible que, pour un cas de diffamation, la police enquête, procède à l'arrestation du journaliste et loge une interdiction de quitter le territoire mauricien contre lui," a-t-il souligné. Manish Gobin dit regretter que l'accès à l'information soit contrôlé dans la Fonction publique et les corps paraétatiques.

Relance du Media Trust

Sur le plateau de Radio Plus, tous les intervenants ont formulé le souhait que le Media Trust soit relancé. « Il faut le réactiver pour assurer la formation des journalistes ," a soutenu Reza Issack. Ce dernier a révélé que le Premier ministre a confié à Gérard Cateaux que le Media Trust serait bientôt réactivé. Cette annonce n'a cependant convaincu personne. Jean-Claude de l'Estrac, de son côté, ne croit pas à un heureux dénouement : « Depuis cinq ans, il a paralysé le Media Trust en ne nommant pas de président. C'est un scandale. Car, chaque année, le Parlement vote un budget pour le Media Trust. » Il dit être arrivé à la conclusion, après réflexion, que la profession journalistique peut avoir recours à la justice pour forcer le Premier ministre à débloquer la situation. Il rappelle que le Media Trust a beaucoup investi dans la formation et qu'une vingtaine de journalistes ont eu la possibilité de suivre des cours de perfectionnement en France.

Le Défi 27/09/2010

Jean-Claude de l'Estrac: « Asphyxier la presse représente un danger »

Lors de l'émission « Pour ou Contre ? », samedi, Nawaz Noorbux avait pour invités Subash Gobine, consultant du Défi Media Group, le légiste Maneesh Gobin, Christina Chan-Meetoo, chargée de cours à l'Université de Maurice et Jean-Claude de l'Estrac, directeur général du groupe La Sentinelle. Il était question des relations tendues entre la presse et le pouvoir.

Le directeur du groupe La Sentinelle, Jean-Claude de l'Estrac, n'a pas fait dans la dentelle. « La meilleure indication vient du Premier ministre lui-même », a-t-il déclaré en faisant référence à une de ses récentes déclarations. « Dans la réalité, l'emballage est de nature politique et idéologique et le moyen utilisé est économique mais la réalité a un sous-entendu communal ," a expliqué Jean-Claude de l'Estrac.

Il a accusé le pouvoir de vouloir asphyxier certains titres de presse et soutenir d'autres. « C'est ça le danger aujourd'hui, c'est beaucoup plus subtil qu'on ne le pense ," a-t-il ajouté. Il avance que si son groupe n'avait pas diversifié ses activités, « l'express » aurait disparu.

Selon Jean-Claude de l'Estrac, les relations presse-pouvoir ont été de tout temps conflictuelles. Il a fait référence aux déboires de la presse sous les régimes de Ramgoolam père, Jugnauth, Bérenger et Ramgoolam fils. « Ils ont toujours agi ainsi car ils pensent que la presse joue contre leurs intérêts ."

Jean-Claude de l'Estrac a également condamné le fait que le Media Trust est paralysé car le Premier ministre n'a pas nommé un président depuis des années. Il n'écarte pas la possibilité d'avoir recours à la justice à cet effet. Le journaliste-parlementaire, Reza Issack, a montré son désaccord vis-à-vis des propos du directeur du groupe La Sentinelle. « Je ne suis pas d'accord que le gouvernement a une stratégie pour asphyxier la presse », devait-il rétorquer.

Il a évoqué une façade qui donne l'impression qu'il y a une

204

relation tendue entre la presse et le pouvoir et que les relations personnelles se seraient détériorées au fil du temps. Il a également affirmé que le Premier ministre n'est pas contre la presse mais contre la publication de fausses nouvelles. Il a cité la manipulation de l'information et des photos surtout durant la période électorale.

« Il y a la guerre et c'est de la bonne guerre ," estime Reza Issack. Il devait avancer que les conflits entre la presse et le pouvoir sont monnaie courante à travers le monde.

Le journaliste parlementaire devait ajouter que si l'on dit que le gouvernement cible certains groups de presse, le contraire est aussi vrai. Il a parlé d'une section de la presse qui cible le gouvernement. « Il y a des membres du gouvernement qui se sentent attaqués ». Reza Issack s'est ainsi dit favorable à une rencontre entre les patrons de presse et le Premier ministre.

Le consultant du Défi Media Group, Subash Gobine, n'estime pas, pour sa part, le gouvernement capable de prendre des mesures pour enlever les acquis des médias mauriciens.

Il a cité les nouveaux médias qui prennent de l'ampleur. D'ailleurs, la presse conventionnelle possède ses sites Web qui diffusent toutes les opinions. « Je ne partage pas le pessimisme des autres journalistes », a-t-il lancé. Pour la chargée de cours, Christina Chan-Meetoo, le gouvernement doit respecter la liberté de la presse pour la bonne marche de la démocratie.

Elle a expliqué que la presse doit elle aussi, de temps en temps, faire son mea-culpa. Si la chargée de cours rejette toute collusion entre la presse et le pouvoir, elle n'est pas non plus d'accord qu'il y ait une relation malsaine entre les deux parties.Christina Chan-Meetoo est d'avis que le gouvernement ne peut museler la presse car cela aura une mauvaise répercussion sur le plan international.

Christina Chan-Meetoo estime aussi qu'une autorégulation de la presse est importante. Mais elle se pose aussi la question sur la formule à adopter. À cet effet, elle a avancé qu'il faut veiller à ce qu'il n'y ait pas de collusion au sein de la presse.

La chargée de cours a aussi rejeté qu'on considère la presse comme le 4e pouvoir. « L'État et la presse ont chacun leurs rôles respectifs », a-t-elle fait ressortir.

Chan-Meetoo considère la presse comme un facilitateur de l'information. « Elle a le devoir d'informer la population aussi bien des bonnes que des mauvaises nouvelles ."

L'avocat Maneesh Gobin a, pour sa part, défendu le droit de l'accès à l'information. Il reconnaît que le journaliste a le droit d'exercer son métier. Il a déploré que l'accès à l'information n'existe pas dans la législation. Il a plaidé en faveur d'une loi qui autorise l'accès du citoyen à l'information, tout comme c'est le cas en Inde. Il a reconnu, toutefois, que des informations relevant de la sécurité de l'État ne doivent pas être divulguées dans la presse.

Le légiste a aussi condamné le fait qu'on favorise certains journaux au détriment des autres titres de presse. En ce qui concerne la désinformation, Manish Gobin a estimé que c'est plus un problème de formation et d'éthique du journaliste.

Parlant de la mise sur pied d'une Media Commission, il estime que ce serait une bonne chose si elle facilite également l'accès aux citoyens pour réparer les torts subis au lieu d'attendre des années pour que l'affaire soit réglée en Cour. Toutefois, il est contre l'idée que cette commission freine la liberté de la presse.

Jean-Claude de l'Estrac: « Je n'ai jamais milité pour une alliance PTr-MMM »

Répondant à une question de Nawaz Noorbux, le directeur général de La Sentinelle a rejeté fortement les allégations selon lesquelles, il a milité en faveur d'une alliance entre le Parti Travailliste (PTr) et le Mouvement militant mauricien (MMM). « Dites-moi quand, où, dans quel meeting, dans quel article de presse, ai-je milité en faveur d'une alliance entre ces deux partis politiques ? ». Il a qualifié ces allégations de fausseté monumentale.

Il devait dire que cette polémique trouve sa source dans une interview qu'il a accordée au « Mauritius Times ." Elle date d'avant les élections. « En répondant à une question, j'ai souligné que malgré les apparences, il n'y a pas de divergences idéologiques entre le PTr et le MMM et qu'il aurait été meilleur qu'ils 'mettent leurs énergies ensemble', pour résoudre les problèmes du pays. Voilà la seule déclaration publique, qui peut de près ou de loin être associée à un voeu d'alliance entre les rouges et les mauves », a-t-il expliqué.

Le Défi 05/10/2010

Me Maneesh Gobin : « La diffamation criminelle peut créer un 'chilling effect' chez les journalistes »

Lors d'un atelier de travail, récemment à l'Université de Maurice, vous évoquiez la nécessité de revoir la loi portant sur la diffamation ? Vous souhaitez décriminaliser la diffamation ?

Oui, effectivement ! Il y a une grande nécessité à le faire. Lors d'un récent atelier de travail, j'ai dit que c'est une des contraintes majeures des journalistes dans l'exercice de leur fonction. Cette infraction de diffamation criminelle, qui existe toujours dans notre Code pénal, ne peut que créer un 'chilling effect' chez les journalistes. Il est inconcevable qu'il puisse y avoir des actions policières contre des journalistes.

C'est ce que la diffamation criminelle permet de faire. Ce 'chilling effect' peut se traduire par une certaine frilosité, qui aura pour conséquence inévitablement un 'holding back' de l'information. Une peur va s'installer surtout si cette loi est utilisée fréquemment par les autorités. Cette nécessité de revoir la loi est reconnue par la Cour européenne des Droits de l'homme.

La Grande-Bretagne a déjà pris des mesures dans ce sens l'an dernier…..

Vous avez raison. Ils ont aboli en novembre dernier la diffamation criminelle, après avoir subi la pression des militants des Droits de l'homme et encore sous les recommandations des personnalités estimées comme Lord Lester et Evans Harris. Du coup, les journalistes peuvent être poursuivis au civil seulement en pas en arrière.

La Freedom of Information Act ne devrait- elle pas être une réalité. Elle ne figure pas Grande-Bretagne. C'est une avancée importante. D'ailleurs, en Grande-Bretagne, depuis des décennies, les dispositions de la loi sur la diffamation criminelle n'étaient pas appliquées. Dans la pratique, elle était déjà obsolète. Ce qui devrait nous amener à réfléchir dans la même direction.

D'ailleurs, l'article 12 de notre Constitution et l'article 10 de la Charte européenne des droits de l'Homme, portant sur la liberté d'expression, est incompatible avec toute tentative de restreindre la liberté de la presse. La diffamation doit être une affaire seulement entre la personne diffamée et celui ou celle qui diffame. Cela ne peut pas être autrement dans une démocratie.

Quelles sont les faiblesses dans les lois régissant la presse ?

Je ne crois pas qu'il faille avoir plus de lois et de réglementations. Les législations existantes sont suffisantes. Je crois toutefois qu'il faut une Media Ombusperson, comme un recours pour le citoyen qui se sent diffamé et qui n'a pas de moyens d'aller en Cour.

Que vous inspirent les nouvelles réglemen tations brandies par les autorités ?

Je ne vois pas un quelconque gouvernement venir avec des lois visant à restreindre la liberté de la presse. Il serait inconcevable, inacceptable et rétrograde de venir avec une telle loi. Maurice est une démocratie mature et je ne crois pas que nous allons faire un tel cette fois dans le discours-programme du régime en place...

La Freedom of Information Act est nécessaire dans toute démocratie respecte. Une des plus grandes démocraties du monde, l'Inde, a une Freedom Of Information Act depuis 2005. L'information est un droit du citoyen. Il est de notre devoir de s'inspirer.

La divulgation des sources d'information reste souvent une problématique. Quelles devraient être les dispositions légales à ce sujet ? Nous n'avons pas de lois sur cet aspect des choses jusqu'ici. Tant mieux ! Mais, les jugements de la Cour européenne sont catégoriques : les sources des journalistes doivent demeurer confidentielles. Sauf pour des motifs très importants, notamment des sujets touchant la sécurité de l'Etat et ayant une grande importance nationale. Mais il devra revenir à une Cour de justice de décider s'il faut le faire ou pas.

www.ingramcontent.com/pod-product-compliance
Lightning Source LLC
Chambersburg PA
CBHW032130020426
42334CB00016B/1112